Robert Collyer

Things New and Old

Sermons

Robert Collyer

Things New and Old
Sermons

ISBN/EAN: 9783743441958

Manufactured in Europe, USA, Canada, Australia, Japa

Cover: Foto ©Lupo / pixelio.de

Manufactured and distributed by brebook publishing software (www.brebook.com)

Robert Collyer

Things New and Old

Sermons

BY

ROBERT COLLYER

MINISTER OF THE CHURCH OF THE MESSIAH, NEW YORK

NEW YORK
E. P. DUTTON AND COMPANY
31 WEST TWENTY-THIRD STREET
1893

Press of J. J. Little & Co.
Astor Place, New York

Dedication

TO THE MEMORY OF THE DEAR WIFE AND MOTHER

CONTENTS.

	PAGE
THE OVERPLUS OF BLOSSOM	7
THE WAY WHERE THE LIGHT DWELLETH	23
MARTHAS AND MARYS	38
THE PARABLE OF THE RESERVES	53
INSTANTANEOUS PHOTOGRAPHS	68
THE LOW-LYING LIGHTS	82
THE CITY LIETH FOUR-SQUARE	95
ANTIPAS, MY FAITHFUL MARTYR	110
THE GREAT DIVINE SERMON	127
WHY SIMON PETER WENT A-FISHING	141
JOHN THE BELOVED	154
SEEING GOD AFTERWARD	167
THE JOY IN HARVEST	181
THE RICH AND THE POOR	195

THE OVERPLUS OF BLOSSOM.

"I see men as trees."—MARK viii. 24.

WE had a cherry-tree once, in our bit of garden out West, which broke out into a wonderful splendor in the spring, and sent its fragrance floating through my study window; but, as I would watch it day by day, I had to remember how it had done this before with no great success in the way of cherries, and then I began to muse over what one might call the overplus of blossom.

I had been away to the South, also, while as yet there were but few signs of spring in the North, and had found this glory haunting the woods and wild pastures and crowning the farms with its beauty; and from this time I had thought of the blossoms sweeping slowly northward until they came to my own window, and covering the land as with a mantle woven of sweetness and light, while, after they had passed our line, I could still see them sweeping northward, and knew they would never halt until they set one lonely bush afire a dear friend of mine found blooming in the hither edges of the arctic circle, as the bush bloomed for Moses in Midian. And then, at last, I knew that, like a great tide, this blossoming would toss its spray over into the lands of utter and hopeless sterility, and touch the moss with specks of blossom as beautiful to those who have the eye to see them as the crowned splendor of the peaches and the apples in the rich, warm lands.

Then my musing blended with old memories, and I found myself wondering whether hosts of children would not fall into the trouble I struck in my own childhood, about the one tree we had which broke out every spring into these extravagant promises of the fruit dear to boys, whose very notions of heaven seem to abide as yet in this matchless liking for what they seem to have liked best in Eden. I wondered whether such boys would not get their first back-stroke, as I did, through their appetite and expectation, and as a great many children do of riper years. That luckless tree never did keep the promise in the summer it had made to me in the spring.

I remember one year especially, after an almost matchless outburst of blossom, how there was the meanest yield of fruit I could remember in my tiny tale of the years; and it was then I said, in some misty way common enough to children who are trying to true the world about them to the world within: "God cannot do as he will, then, or else he changes his mind. He certainly set out to give us all the plums we wanted this year. Now, what does he mean by sending the blossoms and then keeping back the fruit? Would it not be better to do as I would do if I were in his place, —make every blossom stand for a plum, and so save himself and save us also all this trouble?"

After that haggard year I think it was never quite so bad again. There was always a fair show of fruit; and, then, I was getting somewhat used to the frustration. Still, I never could make September quite keep terms with May,— better and worse, but never up to the promises. And so, as I bore the trouble of that tree toward my manhood, and found I had to long for full and plenty of other fruit I must not have, I began to wonder whether it was not of the very exuberance of God's blessing that this overplus of beauty and fragrance comes to us, and whether on the Tree of Life also there may not be a blooming which never comes to anything but the bloom, and yet this in itself may be so good and true that, when we touch the heart of the mystery, we shall neither say, "God has broken his promise to us," nor that we have lost our chance to make this promise good. And as in the spring-time on the trees all about us there are ten blossoms that will bloom through their brief day and then just shower down in the wind to one which will set and ripen into good fruit, so on the tree of my life may there not be ten beautiful aspirations to one good fruition? and yet may not these aspirations themselves be very sweet and good in their own way and be counted as the blossoms are in the glory of the year?

Surely, it must be true that they come as the blossoms come out of the overplus of the divine grace and of our own abounding life, not to dishearten us and lead us to doubt, but rather to believe in this good Providence as insuring us a grand good margin; to believe that God feels toward us as we feel toward our children, when we are good enough and wise enough to be content with such simple and scant fruition as they can attain to, never reckoning with them over-sharply as to what has become of their wealth of good intentions, but listening still with a large and tender interest to the endless story of what they mean to do, and glad to hear about it all because the aspiration is very beautiful to us and very good, even when we know all the time that they will forget ten of these intentions where they will carry one out clear to the end and make it bring forth good fruit.

"Dear hearts," we say, as we listen to them, "it is all right. The blossom itself is fruit in the long fair year of God; and what a wealth of it you have, to be sure. Why, you can intend and aspire enough in ten minutes to ruin you, root and branch, if you should try to make all your intentions and aspirations ripen into good fruit in the seventy years we have for our human span." And so I think it is a good thing for us all, now and then, to turn to this quieter and more restful thought of what we can do within the lines of the truest life, compared with what we can aspire to do, and intend to do, and how we can no more expect or afford to turn the whole wealth of these aspirations into equally noble actions than the trees can afford to make the promise of the spring good to the last blossom in the fruit they will give us in the fall.

Margaret Fuller preserves a letter, written, as I judge, by a woman, who says: "I went this morning to hear Dr. Channing, and came away sadly tired listening to one of his great sermons. He set us up so high, and expected so much from us as the consequence of his doctrine, that, when I got home, I was fain to take my New Testament and read where Jesus says, 'Ye are more than many sparrows'; and the blessed old Word rested me and did me a sight of good, because it was not so exalting and flattering." And I think I can understand that feeling.

The soul cannot live forever in the white light of her own dignity and glory, any more than the sweet wood-violets can live forever in the sun. And so, while it is all true about the dignity of our human nature, and true, also, that no man can ever tell the whole worth of what is waiting in the waiting heavens as the fruit of God's sending and of our own human striving, still that tender glance the woman got through the heart of Christ is very restful and gracious, when we try to measure the distance between the aspiration and the attainment,—"Ye are more than many sparrows." And so you must not be over-troubled, if, while you are quite aware of the wider vision and stronger pinions, you can neither soar so high nor fly so far as your eager hearts would have you. Ye are the branches, and I am the Vine. So bear what fruit you can, then, this year, without damaging the stock for the next.

So I say believe in the trees if you cannot quite believe in yourselves, and note their happy lesson. The blossoms in themselves are good. They mean ten times more than they do; but what beauty and fragrance still abide in their meaning! How it floats over the homes of men as a delicate aroma nothing can slay except the ugly enormity of our overcrowded tenements! So we can thank God for the blossoming in our nature of beautiful and good intentions, which will be sure to fail, as we are taught to think of failing, and for the good fruit, which will be sure to ripen from some of them if we do the best we may.

I. Because this is the first thing to be sure about: that there must be in us all this plus of the promise over the fruition if there is to be any great worth in us besides, and that, in our childhood especially, it may be just this, and very little more, when we are left to live our life as God would have us live it, and when those who have the care of us and love us for ourselves are wise to see how this is about all they can expect from us, exactly as a good pomologist neither looks for nor wishes for fruit from the mere sapling, because he knows how this would fatally injure the tree. So he is quite content, you notice, to see the small things stand there and shake down their blossoms into the grass time and again, and to wait for the fruit by and by.

The strength, he will tell you, is gathering in the roots and the stock, which will come in time to a noble fruitage and repay him for all his waiting. And so it is a sad sight to me to see fathers and mothers who have no such wisdom for their children as these wise men have for the saplings, and cannot be content to let the child be a child, and nothing more, but must still burden the tender plant with demands which belong to the strong and able tree.

Fathers and mothers who are not content to keep the saplings clean from the evil things which burrow around the roots or stab the bole, and to see that the soil is good from which they draw their strength and nurture, keep them straight and true, and then let the sun shine on them, and the sweet dews of their childhood refresh them,— who cannot be content, I say, with all this, and the blossoming into the bargain, but must still be urging them on to fruitful action, while as yet the choicest gift of God to them is this simple aspiration.

Nothing should be expected from these feeble folk save what is perfectly natural (as I think, who have had many children) and fitting for their childhood; and to imagine that they can never begin too soon to assume the cares and burdens of our life, if we can prevent it, is a terrible mistake. The Scriptures say, "It is good for a man to bear the yoke in his youth"; but I would make the yoke easy on the youth God intrusts to me, while on the child it should lie light as the white blossoms on the spray. The best fruitage in children of a tender age is simply to bloom, and to cherish their budding aspirations with the most royal disregard as to what may become of them.

The heaven of our earliest life is white with these blossoms, which are of no use except to sweeten and make more beautiful the way on which we go dreaming in our youth. It is then that the giants are forever slain as they are never slain: and the little hand tingles and aches to get at the wolf, and the small slipper finds the fitting foot, and the cat is the best treasure on the ship, what time the bells have been chiming over Highgate Hill, and the children wander forever through the woods so sweetly forlorn until the bird whose breast became red trying to pluck the thorns from the brow of the blessed Christ comes through the green archways and covers them with leaves.

Leave them to their dreams, I say! Such things are the child's Bible. Leave them to their dreams! These are the blossoms on a tree yielding fruit after its kind, whose seed is in itself. God has made them as they are, in his eternal goodness, as he makes the sapling simply to bloom until the years bring forth strength for bearing. Leave them their childhood sweet and free.

> "They mingle with our life's ethereal part,
>   Sweetening and gathering sweetness evermore,
>   By beauty's franchise disenthralled of time."

II. And, once more, when we grow to that estate in which it is to be expected we shall attain to something more than the tree which blossoms, but bears no fruit at all, you may notice how there is still in many natures, and very often in the finest, a splendid overplus of aspiration and intention which can never be more than as the overplus of blossom on the trees. I suppose, indeed, that now, when the elder men among us have learned some pregnant lessons on this matter, we can still tell of mornings when we would wake up feeling so full of life that we were able to lay out a day's work ample enough to lead us to wonder, as the evening shadows fell, how we could have done so little when we meant to do so much, and were ready to cry with the old Roman, "I have lost a day!"

It is the eternal distinction nature draws between the lusty blossoming and the moderate fruitage, set to the simplest experience and brought within a morning and an evening. But, then, it may be we can see, if we will, now how the overplus of purpose had still this fine quality in it, after all, that we should neither have done so much, nor have done that much so well, had we not risen and gone forth with this fine ambition to be doing boiling in our blood; and it was to the afternoon, when we began to feel the pull of the hard day, what the early rains are to the drought which lasts from mid-

June very often to September, filling all the springs, so that every root gets its share, and the mills are turned by the overplus in the woods and the mountains.

So I imagine it is very seldom possible for those of a hopeful and aspiring nature to make the aspiration and hope of their youth come even with the fruitage of their manhood or womanhood, and least of all in those things which seem quite essential to the fulfilling of their life. Poor Haydon, the painter, I notice, breaks out in his youth into one great cloud of blossoming, when he dreamed he would storm the world by his genius and usher in the new great day of art. But, then, the trouble is this: that the dream of his youth becomes the misery and blight of his age, simply because he never could, or never would, understand this open secret of the overplus of blossom. He did bear some good fruit; and, if he could have said, "Thank God for that: it is the best I can do, and I am content," he might have been a far happier man than he was, and waited for the angels to come and bear him away instead of rushing out of life unbidden and before his time.

And so there are men and women everywhere who, when the strong tide smites them, catch this crown of splendid aspirations and wear it with a great, deep joy. They will write books the world must read, they will create things for which the world will go down on its knees, almost, to thank them, or take a first place in their profession and hold it against all odds, or make themselves seen and heard from an eminence no man may question, or make a fortune no disaster can pluck out of their hands. It is all very good to dream such dreams,—and they may be of a true worth in pushing us on,—only this is the trouble: that I cannot take this truth into my heart, it may be, of ten blossoms to one good apple; and so all my later life is touched with disappointment.

For I certainly have known men whose lives were made miserable by their failure to remember this lesson of the trees. They began their life as if they were quite sure that all they had to do was to just march on and storm the world,—men whose lives blossomed in the early days into the loveliest hopes and aspirations, but who found, when their spring was over, that much of this had come to naught; and then they could not feel that it was a divine thing at all that had befallen them. They imagined a globe would set in every cup and grow and ripen, and so the day came when the sweetness and light of their life left them; nor did they care that even what fruit they had on the tree should find the sun, and ripen the best it might, there seemed to be so little of it, and it looked so mean against the background of their early visions. And so a blight came on their whole career, and that was sour which might have been so sweet and good if they had but known this secret of the overplus of blossom.

III. We may see once more how this lapse between the blossom and the fruit may enter into the whole range of our life, to help us if we will but consider its law, or to hurt us beyond all measure if we will still insist on a fruit for every blossom.

The young man leaves his home in the spring-tide of his life, and feels sure that, if he does his best, he will win a good place and do whatever he hungers and thirsts to do, to find at the end of twenty or thirty years that he is not at all the man he should have been if the fruitage had been equal to the blossom; and, then, he is in danger of growing bitter and doubtful, not about himself alone, but about the good providence of God, which, as he thinks, should have helped him to make his aspiration come true, or else have left him more moderately endowed with aspirations.

Now I would like to get hold of that man, and ask him to note what Nature has been doing in the woods and orchards this year, and then tell him it was a splendid thing to have the aspiration, and that was good fruit, also, of its kind; for if he has been true at all to the inner impulse which crowned his youth with this fair crown, he has done far better than the man who did not aspire and did not care. There is always some good fruit, soon or late, from the blossoming in every one of us,—just as much as we could carry, perhaps, if we could only fathom the whole secret. And so we should no more doubt God's providence because so much of the promise has fallen dead about us than we doubt Nature's providence as she snows down her overplus of blossom about the roots of the trees.

This is the secret, again, of a true content in the life of the heart and the home. For not over many men and women, I suppose, have found that their wedded life answered completely to the dreams of their courtship; but in all the world you will not find a gracious and true-hearted man or woman who will not thank God for that overplus of blossom which came with the sweet, brave days, and was so divine while it lasted, or who will now enter a complaint against Heaven because May does not quite match with October. That fine glamour, if I may touch my figure again, is like great early rains: if they treasure it in their hearts for what it is worth and what it means, it may tide them over many a dry and dusty day, and still keep terms with them that a fair fruitage shall not be wanting when they come to the ingathering of the years.

If my experience is to be of any use, I think a thunder-storm even can do no great harm to this blossoming if it wax not too savage and relentless. I have known such storms clear the atmosphere under the roof about as sweetly as they do above it; and, when I hear of people who have lived together a great many years and never had the least difference, I wonder whether they have not had rather too much indifference for a true man and wife, and am ready to say with Paley, when he heard of such a pair, "It may have been verra bonny, but it must have been a little stupid." God help those who cannot let the fair, sweet bloom go for what it was worth, but must fret their life out over the vanished glory, or poison each other's existence with mutual regret because they cannot live to the end of their days in the sweetness and fragrance of the spring.

It is the lesson we have to learn once more through our saddest and most painful experiences.

Nothing can be more natural and beautiful than that the longing we feel touching the fair blossoming of our children should come to its full fruition, and yet for the most of us this can never be. The bloom fades and falls on which we have set our hearts, that one peerless blossom, as it always seems, we loved best, because it was so beautiful and caught the light so winsomely. The trouble of its falling shakes the soul to its centre, and we often sorrow more for those that have gone than we rejoice for those that abide and fulfil the promises of the spring. It is a long day then, before we can thank God for their blooming that have faded, and say, he did indeed give us the blossoms. They could not stay, but they did come, made May for us in their coming, and left the fragrance of May forever in our life.

Let the trees be my teachers, if I will be taught in no diviner way, and Nature tell me of God's grace if I will not hear the still, small voice. I stood one morning, long ago, by Niagara, in the latter spring, watching the play of the great emerald on the heart of the greater falls as the sun smote it here and there, and the rainbow bent over the eternal white mist. It was a still morning; and, as I stood there, alone, I was aware of an exquisite fragrance stealing across the cataracts I had never noticed in any visit before; and, wondering how this should be, I saw that over in Canada the trees were still all abloom, apple-trees in the orchards and blossoms on the wild bushes clinging to the cliffs, all white and crimson and gleaming through the greenery, and then I knew it was the brave overplus of blossom which was sending its fragrance on the wings of the soft June morning across the great chasm.

And so I have thought of these blossoms which bloom and fall on the tree of our human life and float their fragrance across the turmoil of the days, and across the white mist, and through the bow of our hope. Just a bloom, and no more, some of them, but still a bloom which abides with us while we stay on this side the great river, as that sweet vision abides with me. Shall we not thank God, then, when we come to our better mind, for the blossoms which fall to so divine a purpose? or shall this human sorrow prevent my sense of the divine glory, and my life-long regret for their fading blind me to the divine love which lay in their exquisite advent and grace? I would fain grow great enough, some time, to bless God even for this overplus of life in my home, and think of it as the outpouring of his heart on me for love's sake. I want to grasp a faith which will assure me he could not find it in his heart to give me only children, but would slip an angel, here and there, into my life, in this sweet disguise. These I have with me might well anchor me too stoutly to the earth; but those I *had* with me may draw me wonderfully, if I will let them, toward the heavens where they wait and watch until I come.

IV. And, then, if I turn on myself and say, "What is *my* hope of this blessed life to come, when my life here is but little better than a broken trust, turn where I will, ten resolutions broken where one is made good, the wrecks of undone or half-done duties strewing themselves over the roots of my life, the very hopes and anticipations of the better life not what they were at all in the brave outbreaking of my spring, and my whole manhood or womanhood poor and scant to weeping compared with what I once thought it might be?"

Well, if even this is my trouble, I will not be over-troubled. The splendid hopes and aspirations of the soul's life are all beautiful and all good, as the overplus of blossom, though there be but scant fruit from them, after all, to my poor thinking.

I will tell my heart, then, how God knows better than we know what we are able to bear on to the harvest, what harsh winds also, from which there was no shelter, may have blown on the tree, and what fatalities from the old years before we came here to live our life may have hidden themselves, God help us, in the setting fruit, to smite it with withering.

I will rest me in the parable of the overplus of blossom. I will say, I am more than many trees. I will stand within the law of their life, and they shall stand within the law of mine. I will not be troubled or dismayed overmuch because this poverty has come where I looked for wealth. With these unattained desires and these withered aspirations I will not be over-troubled. I will not give way to despair. I will say to my soul, "If that bush afire with the spring splendor could so storm one poor, halting man in Midian that it seemed as if God spake verily to him out of the bush, and the fruit of that blossoming was for the deliverance of a nation and the help of the world, then my fair hopes and aspirations, which have come to such scant fruitage as I look at them now, may have been fruit in their own time to others who needed just such a pulse of inspiration and aspiration to help them on their way as I had in my nature when it was all radiant with the blossoming of my spring." God knows beyond all my knowing, and he alone can measure the lapse between the blossom and the fruit. Let me stay sweet and trustful, then, and do the best I may on to the fall of my year; and then I will sing,—

> "I know these blossoms clustering heavily,
> The evening dew upon their faded leaves,
> Can claim small value or utility,
> Therefore shall fragrancy and beauty be
> The glory of my sheaves."

THE WAY WHERE THE LIGHT DWELLETH.

"Believe in the light."—JOHN xii. 36.

I REMEMBER how I went once to a fine old city in my mother-land to see many things of a deep interest, and among them the choicest of all was a wonderful cathedral.

It was a dismal morning when I got there, full of mist and rain, through which I could see the church looming up gray with age, but very grand; and there was one window especially which touched me, as I saw it from no great distance, by its splendid outline and the exquisite delicacy of its carven work in stone. I could easily see also from where I stood that this window was filled with stained glass, but it was quite impossible to guess even at the artist's design from the outside, because the background within the church lay in a deep, dense shadow; nor was it meant to be seen in all its fair glory from that side by those who had done the work. It was as if you should look at the wrong side of a piece of tapestry, rude and ragged and all out of true, so there was no form nor comeliness in it as I stood there, and no beauty that one should desire it.

But then I went within the church, and in an instant

was aware of a noble transformation. The soft, misty light came in, revealing the master's intention and clothing all the figures in a dim, gray glory. Still, I remember that even in this there was no great satisfaction. The mist veiled the perfection of beauty, the colors hidden in the glass needed a background of sunlight and a clear sky to come forth in their full splendor; and so I went away.

But about noon the mists rose and were swept away toward the German Ocean, while the sky opened into that tender blue you only seem to see in England in its perfection, like blue eyes dim with tears, through which the sun came out with a mild radiance; and then I went again to see the great window. On the street it was still the same sight, all blurred and blotted, so that the light which lay on it made the figures in the glass seem more uncouth than they were before; but, when I went in again, I saw a great wonder. It was transformed before: it was now transfigured. The whole light of heaven was there for a background, and was smiting the window through and through. There stood the apostles and saints in a great cloud of glory, and above and below them the angels, and all about them the arms and heraldries of men who had given great gifts when the church was built or who had done grand deeds for the nation. Nothing seemed wanting now the heart could desire. The wonderful dyes burned and flamed in the afternoon sun, and the purpose of the master came to me in this fair light of heaven.

And so, as I have thought of this window now and then, among my choicer memories, it has touched me like a bright and cheerful parable of this world of ours, and our life, and of the one true way to find their meaning, so that we shall not doubt or fear finally, whatever may be our fortune, or think of its order and harmony, as I might have thought of that cathedral window if I had still insisted on solving its mystery as I stood outside on the street. Moreover, I have wondered whether the dimness and dismay which trouble us all now and then may not come from our failure to find this true background of the clear heavens and the sun, through standing outside and looking in toward the shadows instead of standing inside and looking out toward the light; and, then, whether we shall not find this truth as the large result of all our seeking,— that those who have found the finest fitness in this life and the fairest hope touching the life to come have always been the men and women who would still insist on finding this fair background for the problems we have to solve, and then on waiting and watching, at any cost, until at last the sun came out to make the whole purpose radiant to them, as my window was radiant in the clear afternoon.

Because, if I may glance first at our common human nature, I think this is what we are sure to find; that there is always a man looking in toward the shadows and another looking out toward the light; and that no single truth we can ponder is more certain than this of the diverse standpoint from which we shall try to make out the mystery of our own life or the lives of those about us. It may be in the nature of the man or in his wilfulness, an inborn quality or one which has grown on him through the years. One can draw no line here, propound no dogma and utter no condemnation, because this human nature of ours is too vast and variant for any private interpretation. And so all we can say so far is this: that one man does insist on setting the design between himself and the fair lights of heaven, while another peers in forever toward the great shadowy vault. And I notice Bunyan thinks there must be a clear purpose to enter where the light dwells, and so to see the truth and grace which will keep you in heart through your pilgrimage; and it may be a certain stern insistence, also, ending in a fight. And so, "Put my name down," he makes the man "of a very stout countenance" say; and then the man puts on his helmet, cuts his way through the guards, presses on toward the house Beautiful, and catches the vision of the eternal day, while the grand old dreamer smiles, and says, "Verily, I know the meaning of this." But, then, he notices also how many give back and will not face the struggle, as if they felt it was not worth their while; and this is the truth, I take it, of the standpoint and the vision common to us all. We nourish this or that spirit and temper, and turn toward where the shadows dwell or the light; and it is as when face answers to face in a glass.

And once more, when we leave this truth as it lies along the great lines of our common life, and notice its special power to help or hinder among those who are our ensample and inspiration, it is not hard to see what worth there is to them in finding this fair light of heaven. We can see how the grand presences which touch us most potently in the Bible are apt to be men of this spirit and temper, from Enoch who walked with

God and Abraham, the friend of God, to that John who stood on Patmos and saw the light which lights the sun strike through the heavy shadows and make all radiant at last down in the mines. It was trouble and dismay and halting to every one of these when they were looking in toward the shadows, but it was a joy which grew into great psalms when they stood at last, as they all do who are of most worth to us, looking out toward the light.

David despairs when he stands, as he does so often, with his back to the sun. Nature is haggard then to him, and life a huge turmoil of selfishness and sin. But he finds his way into some holy place for the soul, and then the harmony masters the harsh discords; and he sings of fire and hail, snow and vapor, summer softness and winter storm all blending together in the great design, and of man so mean and yet made higher than the angels, crowned with glory and honor.

It is Paul's trouble also as he looks in toward the shadows. There is no help then for the sin-smitten race, so chapter after chapter bleeds with disheartenment, woe and pain and utter condemnation. But then he turns to where the light of God's eternal love shines through the blurred and ugly outlines, so dark and forbidding in the fog and mist ; and, lo! the whole design stands forth to his heart in a golden glory as he sings, "I am persuaded that neither death nor life, nor princedoms nor powers, nor things present nor things to come, nor height nor depth, shall be able to separate us from the love of God."

I take it to be the very genius of the Gospels, also,

that Jesus never stands outside, so far as we are concerned, for an instant. But from the day when he takes the lilies and holds them up to the sun, and watches the birds on the wing between himself and heaven,— from that day to the day when he weeps over the doomed city, but still whispers to those about him, "When the worst comes to the worst, then look up," he is always looking toward the light. And so his word still keeps the world in heart, and helps us as no other word can help us to solve the sorest problems of life.

Indeed, you will notice that, when he would touch the one singular instance of this spirit which cannot be content to peer in and ponder, but must always have a background of heaven and the sun, he takes a little child and sets him in the midst, and says, The kingdom of heaven, *the* kingdom, is like that little child. See how the small creature is always looking eagerly toward where the light dwelleth, and so is able to find something of this kingdom in the poor and forlorn life which has fallen to his lot; never trying to spell out the secret from the wrong side; always finding the place where the light will strike through all he can be aware of in the design; familiar with heaven in his simple heart, and glad for it all as a lark in full song, catching the glory and hiding it away for the days when the mists will fall as he stands outside and the glory is only a memory. The little child he will have us see solves the problem of the standpoint for us all. "His angels do always behold the face of my Father"; while Schiller teaches the same truth when he says, "My whole life has only been the interpretation of the visions and oracles of my childhood"; and Wordsworth, when he sings,

"Not in entire forgetfulness,
And not in utter nakedness,
But trailing clouds of glory, do we come
From God, who is our home."

Here is the truth we find in our Bible, then, the book which helps us as no other book can help us,— the word of God,— when we once find the key. The men in there who help and inspire us to the best purpose are those who cannot and will not be content to believe in the shadows, but will have God's presence and his divine providence — *himself*, in a word — for a background to the design ; and for this they will struggle and strive if they must, and wait for the mists to rise and the heavens to grow clear, and then, in Psalm and Prophecy, in Gospel and Epistle, they say and sing these things we hold as the choicest treasure that ever came forth from the human soul.

I notice how this is the truth, again touching those who have done most nobly in helping to reveal the beauty and fitness of the world we live in, and the loftier meanings and outlooks of the life we have to live. It was Newton's turn, who weighed the mountains in the scales, and the hills in a balance. It was old Jacob Boehme's way, who saw heaven as he sat cobbling shoes, and put Newton, it is said, on the track of the infinite order and harmony, and said to John Wesley, by the mouth of William Law, as the great apostle of Methodism, stood looking in toward the shadows: This is no way to solve your problems. You must get heaven's light for your background, and you will find your way out of that dismay. So Wesley heard him, and obeyed,— saw all the wonder of the great design possible to his day, and travelled 40,000 miles to tell what he had seen to those who sat in darkness and the shadow of death. It was their happy fortune; and it was the very soul of Agassiz, who saw heaven through a pebble. That devout and beautiful spirit who, whenever I met him, seemed to be standing with the whole sun in his face, went with the young men to the island the merchant prince, and more than prince, had given them for their summer studies, to spell out the meaning of the shells and rocks, the story of what God has been doing on this earth of ours through a time that smites one like an eternity. And, standing there for the first time, with these eager young souls about him, he said, Let us begin by looking up, each of us in his own spirit, to heaven; while to the end of his life nothing pleased him better than to tell how he had found no trace of the fairer flowers or the birds that make music until he came on the track of man. And so it was to him as if God had said: This child of mine shall look on no desolate and haggard world. I will deck it with beauty and touch it with harmony to meet and clasp the beauty and harmony I have hidden in his heart, and the oriole and the rose shall be to him for tokens of my love.

But Byron said, "I am a torment to myself and to all who come near me"; and it is not hard to see how this should be so apart from the vices that smote his life as with leprosy. Byron, with all his genius, as it seems to me, was forever looking in toward the shadows. And De Quincey says, "I noticed the gloom in John Foster's eye travelling over all things with dismay." Well, this was Foster's trouble: that with all his greatness as a thinker, and his purity and goodness and love for all things good and true, he was always peering in toward the shadows,— human depravity, decrees of doom, hell-fires, ruthless judgments of God, the woful over-weight of sin in the human scales, and other things in the Scriptures no man should dare to take for God's truth as they are commonly interpreted,— peering and pondering as Cowper did so often, and Robert Hall, sometimes dwelling on what Bacon calls the problems dedicated to despair, and preaching,—

> " Like those dark birds that sweep with heavy wing,
> Cheering the flock with melancholy cries."

They are found to be of no use, now, these ponderings and peerings from the wrong side, and only the glances they did compass now and then of the wholeness and beauty of the design, are what we take to our hearts.

So you will notice it is, on the other hand, with the words that win the heart and sweeten and ennoble the life of man. We read the books or hear the discourse of those who are forever looking in toward the shadows,— but there is no rest in them, or help in trouble, or light or joy. We seek bread, and find a stone; break the egg, and it holds a scorpion. We do not take such things to our sick that they may be healed, or pick the kernel out of them for our children. We know where to find the helpful things in the words of those who have seen the light strike through the mystery, and take these for the need we all strike soon or late. The men and women who stand in the front rank of our religious teachers and thinkers — not to sects alone, but to the nations — are those always who look out toward the light and hold it in their hearts. Emerson, Bryant,

Longfellow, Lowell, Whittier, Channing, Parker, Bellows, Beecher, Clarke, and a host besides, to speak only of the noble dead,— it is one golden chain from Alpha to Omega. The words which bring their own benediction come home to us from those who have stood in the holy place and seen the light strike through, to find this as the last great word: God is light, and in him is no darkness at all; and God is love. Such is the truth, as it comes to me, of fronting the light; and now these are some of the lessons we may gather from it to help and hearten us.

Does my life, as I must live it, trouble me? and my fortune? Are these all a muddle, as poor Stephen says in the story? Then I must lay this truth well to my heart: that the men who win are very seldom those who are always peering and pondering on the dark side. They are those who get heaven and the sun for the background to their own best striving; and then the fairest fortune possible to us comes through that winsome light. To lose this is to lose my strongest ally, and I put a cheerful courage on when I stand with my face to the sun. The successful men in the long fight with fortune are the cheerful men, or those, certainly, who find this fair background of faith and hope. Columbus but for this had never found our New World, or men like Sam Adams struck the bell for the Revolution in the great old days.

Is there trouble again with that which lies deeper? Are my health and strength in peril? Well, I think there can be little doubt of this: that those who are forever looking on the dark side of their illnesses and ailments, peering in toward the shadows when they should face the light, toss away the finest chances left them to get well again ; while those who strive for a cheerful background of faith and hope either win health or, if this is not to be, win some high blessing which may come by sickness.

There is an excellent satire under the cap and bells when the doleful doctor comes to see his patient, and says sadly to the poor man, There is not one chance in a thousand that you will get well, but I commend you to be cheerful. I want no such Jeremias when my turn comes to be sick, but men who will bring me all the good cheer in the world in their eyes and the tones of their voice and the touch of their hand, and will say to me, While there's life, there's hope, my friend; and I propose to help you get well. A dear friend of mine used to say of a fine old doctor in Philadelphia that his simple presence did his patients more good than his medicine, and was easier to take beyond all comparison. This was forty years ago. Well, such a presence is always a noble medicine in itself. The contagion of a cheerful soul helps us always to look toward the light, sets the tides of life flowing again, and cubes all our chances of getting well. It was a very common grievance among the surgeons who had this good cheer in them, when we used to leap out to nurse our men after the great battles, that well-meaning but woful-looking men of the old school — in theology, I mean — would invade the hospitals and rob the brave fellows of what courage was left in them by the dolor of their words and the sadness of their presence, when the delicate balances between life and death drew about even, and not seldom would turn the scale for death. I want no such curate for mind or body, no such doctor or nurse or priest. They must come as the good Christ came,—for healing, and not for affright. 'Tis life of which my nerves are scant then; and, if they have no ministry of life unto life, I can wait until some cheerful soul comes to give me a hand.

Has that trouble smitten me for which I think there is no healing? Are those who were the very light of my life taken while I am left,— the lambs in the flock, the youth in its fair bloom, the manhood or womanhood in its perfect prime? It is a great and sore trouble. God forbid that I should say otherwise. How can I? and, if I could, Jesus would rebuke me, weeping beside a grave. But may not the trouble within the trouble for the most of us be this: that we look in toward the shadows so ruthlessly, stand with our back to the sun, peer into the vault, nurse our vast and awful sorrow, and let this make havoc of us beyond all measure, instead of trying to find the place where the sunlight of the immortal life will smite through the trouble, and stir us to a new hope and expectation? The one true way, I will tell my heart then, is to set our graves even against this background of heaven and the great and sure hope of man. Good Bishop Horne says, Wormwood eaten with bread is not bitter. Well, let me eat my wormwood, then, with the bread of life. here have been and are those who find the place where the light strikes through the grave,— yes, the very grave,— and then the whole haggard and hopeless sorrow suffers a change. So we must try to find that place, too, who sit in darkness and the shadows of death. There may be many things we cannot make out after all, as there was to me that afternoon in the great window; but the light is there, burning through and this is the grand matter. Death has no dominion when we once find the place where a sure faith and a great hope in God can smite through these vast, sad shadows of death and the grave.

So, if the truth stands good, finally that some will be forever looking toward the shadows, while others will never be content until they find where the light dwelleth, let us, please God, be of these last. Those great souls of the old days and the new who help and inspire us to the finest purpose and the most divine have caught the secret of the true standpoint for you and me. Let me stand where they stood, fronting the light. Then it shall smite through sickness for me, and pain, and the dark glass of hard fortune, and make a nobler faith my own in life and death. Let me try to do as they did. Be wilful about this grand matter,— be cowed by no rebuff, tired out by no waiting, and beaten in no fight.

"Here is the rock," they said to me, when I was up among the miners, "and here is the gold, and we pursue it through thirty-six processes; but there it is, you see, at last. Heft that bar, sir." So wilful would I be for this clear shining of God's resplendent sun, for this fine gold of his truth,— waiting, watching, and searching for it as those who search for hid treasure. I think the main trouble with my doubt and dimness is this: that I do nothing about it, but let them have their way, it may be, who tell us there can be no light on these misty mysteries. I may have been all too ready to fall in with such a conclusion and to stay outside. Let me go into the holy place, and hear Him who said so grandly, "I am the light of the world," and has proved his word to be so grandly true in all these ages, then I shall not abide in the darkness, but shall have the light of life.

Do I find this mist troubles me as I stand at the portals of life, and wonder how I shall win through. I will front the light. Do I find dimness in age, let me explore old Bunyan again, and have him tell me how those that fared on toward the end of their pilgrimage, faithful and true, came at last to where the sun shineth alway. Nay, is my faith itself in the shadow,— not lost, but in the mist,— then let me sing with the fine old Wesleyan heart in me I caught from her nurturing, "In hope against all human hope, self-desperate, I believe,"— sing until the sun comes out as I watch and wait, and hasten his shining by my singing. Nothing shall withstand my hungry wilfulness to front the light. I also will say, "Put my name down, sir: I mean to go in there, and face the glorious appearing"; and the old dreamer shall say of me, also, as he watches me from his hard-won eminence, "Verily I know the meaning of that." For

> "Two powers, since first the world began,
>   Have ruled our life, and rule it still.
>   Twin forces in the life of man
>   Are Faith and Will.
>
> "The pole-star and the helm of life,
>   That sets the head, this gives the force,
>   Through seas of peace, or stress and strife,
>   To shape our course.

"These powers which stand in God's own strength,
 In dark and light, in joy and doom, —
 Unshaken are the powers at length
   That bring us home.

"But where is home? That faith can tell.
 But what is faith? That will can prove
 In striving bravely, working well,
 And fronting God's eternal love."

MARTHAS AND MARYS.

"Mary sat at Jesus' feet and heard his word, but Martha was cumbered about much serving."— LUKE X. 39, 40.

IT was in Bethany these good women lived, as we learn from the Gospel by John,— an obscure place not far from Jerusalem, on the eastern slope of the Mount of Olives, where the road to Jericho dips suddenly toward the Jordan. And it is a pretty spot, those say who have been there, in a hollow of the slope, planted thick with fruit-trees, but otherwise of no account; for it is peopled by some twenty families as thriftless and shiftless as you will easily find, who live, as so many seem to do in the Holy Land, by the lies they tell about the so-called sacred places. Nor can the place have ever been of much account; for it is not once mentioned in the Old Testament, and there are no signs that the hamlet ever overflowed the small cup in which it stands.

This, again, was no formal visit Jesus made there, that the scene might be painted in the panorama of his three years' pilgrimage, so that the small place in the hollow of Olivet should be lifted into the light forever, like Bethlehem spoken of by the prophets and ordained to shine. He was on his way to Jerusalem. These were his friends, the sisters and the brother; and he must stay with them, as their guest, it may be, for the night, — a guest greatly honored and most welcome as we can see, to whom they will give the best they have, and to the friends who have come with him. And this must be done by the two sisters; for the brother is not mentioned here, and may have been away from home. And one of them loses no time, it is clear, touching the hospitable purpose which stirs her heart. She is, indeed, the owner of the place, and so it rests with her to see to it that the best is set on the board she has in the house; while I think of her as one of those clever and capable women who can never be taken at a disadvantage in such a case as this, but can surprise those who have known her longest and best by the way in which she will call out her reserves. It is her purpose to do this now. You can see her rise to the rare occasion, think it over to herself for a moment or two, and then brighten up as she gets out her keys and moves swiftly about the house. It is a lovely little picture, and human, as we watch the good woman, and good housekeeper to the last line. They shall remember their visit as one of the events of a year or a lifetime, and shall fare well before they say farewell to go on their way.

But just here she falls on a trouble. Mary, her sister, and no doubt as good as gold in such a case usually, fails the good Martha now, when she needs her most. It was the most natural thing in the world that she should be as busy as her sister was. So you would have felt in Martha's place,—the Marthas in my congregation. The good name of the house was to be maintained, and due honor done to the guests by good and loving service. But, while she also is busy, as we may presume, helping Martha, Jesus begins to speak of the things which always lay so deep in his heart,— how the kingdom of God is as leaven, it may be, when they began to make the bread, and as old and new wine, touching these homely things for divine lessons. We do not know what he said, only that Mary sat at his feet and listened, while poor Martha had everything to do, first to make ready and then to serve.

Nor can we easily believe that the good Martha gave up without giving Mary what we should call a piece of her mind in frowns and whispers before she was driven to the last extremity, and would have to shame her before the whole company; for this would be as natural as all the rest. She was sharp, to be sure, for this they say is implied in her name, and could be a little more than sharp, as our Marthas are apt to be before time mellows them and makes them sweet,— time and the grace of Heaven. But, if this was so, it was all no use. Mary sits still and listens, and is lost to all that is going on about her; and then the much tried woman makes her appeal to the guest and friend: "Dost thou not care that my sister hath left me to serve alone? *Bid* her, therefore, that she help me." While it is the surmise of a rare scholar and seer I love to follow that there is a touch of desperation in this swift and keen appeal of kin to that of the disciples in the great storm,— "Carest thou not that we perish?" In any case, she will be patient no longer, or keep her impatience to herself. She must speak out.

Nor is the surmise poor or thin that Jesus had not

noticed the sister's trouble at all down to this moment, or thought it strange that Mary should not be busy with her sister, or been aware, indeed, of what was there before his eyes. It was one of those high moments when his meat and drink was to reveal the truth which had come to him instantly from on high, as it was when he sat talking to the woman by the well; and then, when they brought him bread, he said, "I have bread to eat ye know not of."

In the great and moving moments in our own lives we can all tell how we were lost to the things about us,— lost in the vision, so that we forgot the needs of the body and the passing of time. So it may have been, and so I think must have been with him that day. But now here was Martha with her cutting question, "Dost thou not *care* that my sister hath left me to serve alone? Bid her, therefore, that she help me." And then, in an instant, he would see where the trouble lay and how to meet it, but not as she would think he would meet it,— the good and loyal friend of overburdened men and women, who made their trouble his own. This trouble was of quite another tenor from those that always moved his heart to pity and swift succor. This good friend, with the best of all good will in her kindly and hospitable heart, had got herself snared in a net of her own netting: she was careful and troubled about many *things*. Very good things, and needful there and then as she thought, but quite at the other pole of our human life and duty as the question touched him that day, and as it may touch us now. Many THINGS,— social duties, hospitable aspirations, kindly endeavors, and the best she had for the best she knew. These friends who were living very much as the birds live were to be ministered unto by one good meal. They were men friends, and therefore in the more need of her ministry,— men friends and ministers of the word of life, and therefore to be cared for, so she had been taught from her childhood, no doubt, with all the more care and pains. It is a sweet human picture, as I said, when you wipe the dust of the ages away, and restore the lost lines; and who shall blame the good Martha for her touch of temper and her half-command, "*Bid her*, therefore, that she help me"? He does not blame her, but, as I listen, there is a tender, lingering, loving kindness in the repetition of her name even, as he says, "Martha, Martha, thou art troubled about many things; but one thing is needful." He would not rebuke: he would only help her to see where the truest hospitality lay,— and do this not as the Master and Lord, but the good friend and guest. And so I think we do him dishonor when we give his words another and harsher meaning.

Nor should we lose track of the simple and quite human purpose which prompts the divine lesson he would suggest to his over-troubled hostess and good friend. We all know how it would touch him when he saw what her trouble was, who have gone to the home of some friend in very much the same way,— not, it may be, expected, but right welcome all the same. When we have had to notice how full of care the house-mother was about our handsome and fitting entertainment, we wanted to say: Do sit down, and take no thought of what we shall eat or what we shall drink. We have come to see you all, and here are so many things we all want to say,— books to mention, events to discuss, memories to brighten, hopes to touch, deep things and high to wonder over,— and it may be now or never. And so what can a feast of fat things and wine on the lees well refined be to such a communion of the spirit and the life? Bring out the loaf and the cup, as if you had no guests at all, and do not be cumbered by much serving. We will serve ourselves. So it must have been that day. He was no anchorite, as we know, but would go to a feast on occasion, and had no rebuke for the good woman's feast now. But there sat the sister she had scored with her sharp tongue, listening to the word borne into his heart that instant from on high,— the bread of life and the water of life,— the word made flesh and dwelling among them from sunset to gray dawn, and the word which was to lie within the heart of a new gospel; not his word, but the word of the Father which sent him, and he was speaking to him then. So Mary must be vindicated, and the sting drawn from the good sister's rebuke. She was true to her own soul and the soul of the truth and the time. This was the event of a lifetime, and, while she did not know it, the lifting of the home in the hollow into a light that never lay on land or sea; and so, he said, Mary hath chosen that good part which shall not be taken from her.

So the story of an evening opens to my mind as they sit there forever now, the Master and his friends; while the one sister hurries about the house so intent on serving, and the other sits still listening to his words who spake as never man spake, and as one having authority, not as the scribes. In a paper I took up the other day a rustic tells how he would be busy about his farm or hurrying on an errand, when one of the last age who was also filled with the Holy Spirit would walk along the green lane by the Lake in Westmoreland, unaware of any other presence, saying words fresh from the fountain of the divine inspiration that hold so many of us now by their sweet, strong spell. But all the listener could do was to wonder how a man so able otherwise could spend his time talking in that way all to himself, and to a far poorer purpose than if he had been repeating the multiplication table, or in any sense so fitting as what the parson said on Sunday in the queer old church. One has to wonder whether our good Martha had not some such feeling about the high discourse that fell on her ear, as the rain falls on the water fowl, while she went about the house with the chicken and omelet and the fine wheaten cakes and the milk and honey on her mind, glancing at her sister and glowering, as we used to say in the north, until she can no more help that sharp word than our good friend Mrs. Poyser can in the story,— the perfect Martha of her day and generation. It was Martha's opportunity, also, to hear the word, and we hear in a casual way from other quarters that she was a good, sound churchwoman and much given to listening to the holy men in the synagogue on Sunday and to good works; and we may be sure of the good works even more than of the listening, especially if there were signs that one of the hives would swarm before the holy day was over or the thunderous weather turn the milk.

But this was a week-day, and here were the guests, these good men and the Master, who so seldom had a good meal set before them; and what discourse ever was so momentous to Martha as this social and, to her mind, most sacred obligation? So they are own sisters, and no doubt true and loving sisters, but with this diverse temper of the heart and mind when we catch this swift glimpse of them in the hollow of Olivet: The one quiet as a Quaker and content to sit still this one evening, whatever she may do to-morrow, and sun her soul in the light fresh from heaven; the other busy as a whole swarm of bees, and ready to "bizz out wi' angry pyke," while the words fall from his lips she would give the world, no doubt, to hear, when so many years after she is an exile in the South of France, so say the traditions, for love of him. She loved him in her own way when she turned on him and said, "Dost thou not care that my sister hath left me to serve alone? Bid her that she help me." And the same Martha in the Legends again as she is in the Gospels; for she slays a dragon,— a thing Mary never would have done,— a noisome and ugly thing which was devouring the children in Marseilles,— an evil marsh, I take it, or the mother of all bad drains,— with diphtheria and the scarlet fever; for it takes Martha to do that, after all.

Shall I say once more, then, that it is no wonder the Fourth Gospel, and the last in the divine series, tells us how Jesus loved *Martha and* Mary, and mentions the good and true woman after her type first, as if the Holy Spirit had held the pen this instant, as indeed it does in many instants now, and would make her this amends for the half-bitter word she said this day, and the injury done to herself for so good a reason as her temper and disposition ran toward all generous and hospitable ends? And shall we not say, as we leave her wondering over the Master's words, and half inclined to cry,— for the tears are very near the eyes with the Marthas,— that we must not wonder the divine heart in him who knew what was in man and woman should still go out to this capital and much cumbered woman, so anxious about the duty and grace of hospitality and of good house-*keeping;* the crown and glory of her life and of her ancient Scriptures, and say also for her vindication, as we note her worth, What would the world be without our Marthas, who cumber themselves so sore, and very much as she did, by much serving? Who are so noble, indeed, and capable to take care of themselves in our modern life that they need no advocate; but the Marys rather need one, as she did who sat at the Master's feet in the old time, and was lost in his word. In this modern life and the life in this fervid centre, especially, where not to be a Martha, when the demand is on you to see well to your home and your social duties, is to be next of kin to nobody among the good women of our city, and of Boston, let us say with a slightly deeper emphasis, this is the canon of our womanhood,— to stand by Martha; while of our manhood it may be,— for I would walk delicately here, the less I say, the better. Still, is it not true that we all want these Marthas to look after us rather than the Marys,— to see, as the older Scripture says, that we are honored among the elders in the gate if the years have told on us, or, if we have to make our way up the ladder, to be our help-meet and lend a hand as we climb, and so make good the axiom that the man must ask his wife how far up he shall go? We love to see the home crisp and bright as a new-minted dollar, and to see the house-mother rise to the level of the swiftest demand when the guests come in, or we bring them in, even at the cost of that sharp word now and then, which is not for the sister or the guests, and, if we are not mere clowns, and no gentlemen, enjoy it perhaps, as we enjoy the blowing of the west winds these spring days, but take care not to say so, while it well contents us, take us in the mass, to hear how the Marys, who have only this fine grace for their gift,— to be still now and then, and listen, and, it may be, speak or write, — how they cannot hold a candle to the Marthas in the social or the housekeeping life, and are of quite no account so far in the town or the country side.

The Marthas, then, need no advocate in the life we are living, with its crowded hospitalities and thick-sown social duties; but, then, we have to ask the question I have answered in part already,— whether this is true of the Marys, of whom it was said they have chosen the good part which shall not be taken from them. Is this the better part on which so many of us, men and women alike, have come to set such store in these times, or in any time? Have they struck the great key-note of life in France, let us say, for an instance, where they are so proud of the capacity and quality of the woman in the home, in society, and in business,— the matchless Marthas, so clever and capable that the men folk, as you used to call them in New England, are content to be ciphers very often to their unit, and only to plume themselves on their Panama canals and copper trusts, in which they waste what the Marthas have made? If I have learned the mere alphabet of a true and noble life, I say No to such a conclusion now and forever, and stand by His word who said, Mary hath chosen the good part, when she had caught the great and high moment on the wing and sat at his feet, content to drink in the divine word fresh from heaven, and let all else wait or be blown down the wind, if it must be so, for that great golden opportunity to see far into heaven. In the old time, when the highest things came to us on the bee-line, as they come still to our children, the holiest and highest came not through the man, but the woman; and this was especially true of the Greek and Roman and the race to which we belong. It is the bud to the blossom. It is the fruit to the vine. It is the alphabet to the Bible in this truth I want to touch, — the truth that not the priest, but the priestess, is the grand factor in the diviner life of man now; and the Marys, not the Marthas, that we must look to for the highest and the best,— of whom we have to ask the question, How high shall we go? I allow the claim gladly of her sister's energy and faculty, and all noble qualities beside that belong to her nature; but all the same I say of Mary, She hath chosen that good part which shall not be taken from her. The home, the church, the city, and the republic, and the world all around wait finally for the Marys rather than the Marthas, so far as the woman has her portion and lot in its highest and truest life,— the woman and womanhood of the deeper heart and vision whose life is hid with Christ's in God.

It came to me to think and speak of this again through the sudden hush, over which I never cease to wonder, which falls on the Marthas when Lent * comes

---

* Lent, 1890.

round among those who stand within the lines of the Roman and Episcopal Churches especially, and in one way or another touches us all. There has been no such devouring hospitality since I came to live in New York as I have noticed this winter, or such dissipation of life,— I use the word in no evil sense,— in which they have had to bear the main burden; and not seldom I have heard the longing expressed that Lent might come, and then they would be free from this cumber of much serving as hostess or guest. It is a wise and gracious provision of these great old churches for the Marthas of their fold. No more of that, they say. For forty days you must sit down, also, with the Marys now, and listen to the word from on high. The channels of your life must be deepened and cleared of the sand, so that the waters may run sweet and clear. *Hear the Church.* It is our habit to smile at this, and congratulate ourselves that we are under no such bondage; but may we not ask, as we do this, whether it is not freedom to great hosts of Marthas who have been wearing their lives out and their souls away in what they call their social duties,— this first, and then, what is better still, if they are true to the primitive intention of the holy time, the sitting down with Mary and letting the heavy care go by of so much serving, while they open their heart to higher and better things, and have some crumbs of the good part which shall not be taken from them, so that their life shall not be like the river I saw in the Far West,— a long drift through the dry desert,— to be lost finally in the sands and create only a marsh,— the Humboldt sink they call it.

The thought of the sisters touches me also to this

closer purpose, that those who hear me shall mind this truth from the Master's lips. It is the natural instinct of our finer womanhood to range with Martha, and be like her, as it is the drift of the time. To be clever and hospitable and able, not seldom to hold your own in the world's business as well as a man, or to surpass many men,—in this I have taken pains to mark my admiration of Martha; But, as I think of the ever-growing tendency to be cumbered about many things, as she was, and note the multitudes of women so cumbered, I wonder where the Marys are, and how many of them are left of this nobler mind and purpose,—maidens who will not give all their time to the world's ways and fashions, or to light and frivolous reading and the charm of light conversation, or to running hither and yonder on vain and empty errands, or even to more serious things that still go only to the making of Marthas, but will have their time for listening to the diviner voice, the still, small voice, the whisper of the Holy Spirit of God. And women in the heart of the world's life who find they must nourish the deeper heart of Mary while their lot lies greatly with Martha,—and it may be their temper and disposition also,—that they may not only save their own souls alive, but be help-meets, indeed, to those of us who are as the life of their life, and who, it may be, can only climb the ladder which reaches toward heaven as they stand on the step above us and hold out their hand, and who will say to the children what He said who took them in his arms and blessed them, and then make it all come true,— of such is the kingdom of heaven,—how many are there? Many, many, many, or our life in this New World holds no great hope for man. Clever as they are and good as gold, these good Marthas, the saving salt of the noblest and best, the deeper heart and devout and reverent is not in them as it was in the primitive mothers of the nation; and we must have women like these and like Mary always.

Many such women there are, as my faith runs; and my sight now and then confirms my faith. Lucretia Mott was one of them,— as good a Martha as the world held in her time, but then, also, as good a Mary. The home kept perfectly, the children trained beautifully, and all living their own lives well, the social duties which must be observed all kept up to the line, everything of that sort well done; but, then, this also, the quiet inward life kept sweet and free to hear the word, deep thoughts of the heart coming and going in communion with the highest, the few choice books, heart books, read and read again, and a glance of the eye toward all the great and hopeful movements in the world's great life.

Elizabeth Gaskell, also, the busy pastor's wife in Manchester, with a great parish on her hands and wide-reaching social and home duties of every sort,— a perfect Martha, as I found her once,— yet also, if we may judge, a perfect Mary, sitting at the Master's feet and listening, and writing "Ruth" and "Mary Barton." Martha could not write them, only Mary. And so it is, and has been always.

It is what I plead for in this Lenten sermon; for why should we not also hear Lenten sermons? I would begin at the beginning, and this is with the Marthas and Marys. Shall we ask what the next age will be, we must not ask the men of this age, or the ministers, or the schools even, and colleges. We must ask the maidens and wives and mothers, and the womanhood all round, the Marthas and Marys apart or in one. They hold the casting vote for goodness and righteousness and truth; and you who hear me are among them, to whom Paul also said, "Be not conformed to this world, but be transformed by the renewing of your minds, that ye may know what is the good and acceptable and perfect will of God."

THE PARABLE OF THE RESERVES.

"But the wise took oil in their vessels with their lamps."—MATT. xxv. 5.

THE parable of the ten virgins is, on the whole, a sad story. You do not care for the one-half of them the instant after they enter the door,— or before they enter, for that matter,— when once you find them out, and take note of what seems to be their utter selfishness. Your heart stays outside with the five who are peering in through the windows, listening to the music and weeping while the others are dancing. You say, It is too bad, and would fain open the door and let them in also; while you wonder why the bridegroom is not of your mind, and begin to make excuses, and to find reasons for a fairer conclusion than this which is written. There was no harm in them, you say. They were only thoughtless, and even this might come in such a case through their eager haste to be on hand. This would be in itself a fine trait. Or their lamps may have gone out through the boundless generosity of their burning, while those of the other five were kept alive by parsimony in the use of the oil, as well as the forethought which provided a reserve. At any rate, you would like to know the rights of all this before you make up your mind to leave these poor damsels to their distraction. And, even if you were sure it was a just judgment, you would still owe those insiders a grudge for not squeezing out a few drops at least to help their sisters up to the door, at some risk to their own lamps, so that they might all go in or stay out together. Or, what would be well worth the trying, trust that on his wedding day, at any rate, the master of the feast would be of a generous mind, and say, Come in, every one of you, when they all came in the dimness to the door, and told him how it was no use thinking of leaving the one-half there on the street to take their chance at the closed doors, so their lamps had *all* gone out through a motive they were sure he would admire above all things in his own wife.

Neither are you satisfied with the way in which the parable is commonly made to open toward our life and its outlooks hereafter. In the German there is a story of Frederick, Margrave of Misnia, who in 1322 went to see one of the old Mystery Plays drawn from the parable, in which the five wise virgins were the noblest women the playwright could imagine. But they had grown hard and stern as fate to their hapless comrades, and left them easily outside weeping and wailing, which, when the prince saw, he was so amazed that he fell into a grievous sickness, crying, What is our Christian faith, then, and love? died on the fourth day after, and was buried at Eisenach. And we are very much of the Margrave's mind. If our faith means anything, we say, worth the name, it means that we shall help each other when the pinch comes, at any cost, and grow rich by giving rather than by hoarding; while about the meanest thing a man or woman can do is to nourish the idea of crowding into whatever bliss may be awaiting, no matter who may have to stand outside, and having your fill of joy while your old comrades are in despair.

It is a fair objection, born of all that is most generous and noble in our human nature, and by consequence most divine. It seems as if such a selfish spirit would make heaven itself anything but welcome to those of wider sympathies and a deeper pulse of grace, when they found themselves in such company. And so these interpretations are rejected as unworthy the grand and generous soul of the gospel of the Son of God. But I think the truth is that we fall into this trouble and many more of this kind through our misconceptions, and say one thing when our great Teacher means another. So it is of the life to come he is speaking here, the commentators say; yet, when you read what precedes and follows the parable, you find it is not the life to come which is in his mind then, and least of all our notions of that life, but the life right there they had to live in those days and we have to live now, with its outlooks and inlooks, and the kingdom of heaven is no far-away world among the lights and shadows of eternity, but the life of God in human souls on this earth, while even then it is not that life as we insist on it in our sermons and systems, but the widest and deepest relation of man to

God we can imagine, meeting us at every turn and keeping the record of all we do.

This is the way, therefore, the parable I want to touch opens to my mind. There was trouble in the air as Jesus was speaking. He saw it through his divine insight; while those about him still felt safe and sure of their lives and fortunes, and would not be disturbed of their rest. It is coming, he tells them once and again, as a thief in the night; and no element in it, as he foresees, will be more terrible than its surprise. It will be like a thunderbolt out of a clear sky, like the swift agony of fire in a sleeping city, like the spring of a wild thing as you walk without a fear through the quiet glades of a forest, like all great trials now and forever, when you least expect them.

Then he foresees how there will be a division among those who spring out of the slumber to meet the demand of the day and night,— how some will have reserves of light and life and the power to hold their own, while others who have no such reserves will have to give up and lose their place, submit to the loss, and stand outside; while this must all come to pass through a law of life against which there is no appeal and for which there is no help save through seeing to the reserves of oil in good time, and so being prepared for the demand when it comes suddenly on all alike There may be the best desire in the world on the part of those who are ready to help the rest who must fall back; but there is no margin, and so no way. The reserves must be there ready to meet the demand, then the end of it all will be glory and honor; but not there, it is too late to create them, and the end is disgrace and shame. It is not a question of sentiment, therefore, but of life in its solemn ordeals, and not so much of the way we shall win into heaven as the way we shall live, first of all, to the truest purpose on the earth.

So, when we set the parable in this light, it is not hard to see how it enters into our own life and time, and brings the truth home no man can afford to neglect,— the truth that we must also have the reserves to fall back upon when the demand comes, or we can never spring forward to any great purpose,— Reserves of life or light, of courage or character, of insight or endurance, or of whatever the demand may be; for, failing here, it is as when the wells fail in a dry time because they have no deepness or power to reach the perennial springs.

In our common life we may do as well as those about us, or seem to be doing better, even, if we are reckless about the reserves, while others are carefully storing them away. But the truth is, such times are no test of the man and manhood any more than the piping times of peace, when they flame out in scarlet and gold in London, are a test of the queen's guards, or than our own men were tested when they marched southward through our streets with their music and banners. It is Waterloo and the Crimea, Chancellorsville and Ball's Bluff, and such grim backgrounds as these, against which they must stand before the matchless manhood can come into high relief and reveal the truth of the reserves. And so we can all go easily enough through our own easy-going times, make good headway, as we imagine, and hold our own with the best, while such times hold no virtue in them to bring out the reserved power.

They are like the main part of a voyage I made once across the Atlantic, in which the weather was so pleasant and all things ran so smoothly that I suspect the most of us felt we were about a match for the captain, and concluded it was no great thing, after all, to run a steamer, when you once got the lines. But a great storm struck us as we were nearing Cape Race, and all night long the good ship shuddered and panted through the mighty billows or over them; and when next morning, peering deckward, we saw our captain standing by the main mast, his arms twisted about the ropes, swinging in the tempest and watching it with steady eyes, alert and cheerful, though they told us he had been on deck all night,— turning his vessel round in the thick of the tempest and the trough of the sea, so that she might escape the awful strain and the avalanche of waters which were filling many with dismay,— then we knew our captain. The reserves were shining out. Here was a man no storm could daunt, and who, if the worst had come, would no doubt have been the last to leave the ship. That man had light in him and life equal to the demand,— oil in the vessel with his lamp; and so he brought us to the desired haven.

I. Now this demand, when we bring it home, touches, first of all, our life itself. For your wise doctor will tell you that about the best thing you can do is to keep as fine a reserve of vitality as you can possibly store away, if you mean to give him a chance when some day he has to help you pull through in the sore conflict between life and death to which we are open, exactly, perhaps, when we least expect it. And how many times we have all heard that same sad story! Nothing could be done for him, because there was nothing to fall back upon. He had no reserve of power to fight through: he used up all his life as he went along. And that most cheering story, on the other hand: He was about as sick as a man can be to live; but he had a splendid constitution and great reserves of power, and so he pulled through. Here, then, is the first meaning of oil in my vessel with my lamp, as it lies in my very life. I can be wary and foreseeing about this blessing on which all other things I can be and do down here must rest; and then, when the last stern test comes, it is as if so many more strands were cabled about the one slender thread. So many a life has ended all too soon through what we call a mystery of providence, when the most heedless and reckless improvidence has really used up the reserves; and so we should be careful how we use such a term or go after a mystery while the simple truth waits right under our eyes. We use up these reserves, and are smitten by a sickness which would draw on all our powers if we had kept them stored away, but they are wasted; and then I speak as a man when I say that the Eternal God is as powerless to pull us through as the good doctors are, while, if it were otherwise, we can imagine no greater misfortune, for we should all turn spendthrifts in the assurance of getting a renewal. There is no such subtle temptation to improvidence as that which lies in the feeling that the high powers will suspend the law if we do but cry loud and long enough.

And still another truth waits to be touched before we pass this first line; this, namely, that these reserves of life mean more than mere living. They mean what the Master hinted at,— an enduring brightness breaking into joy, because the man who has the most life, and still knows how to use and store it, has usually the most worth of life. The grace and glamour of existence come of the overplus of oil. Show me a man who is running forever on a close margin, and I will show you a man who has more than his share of dark, grim days, one to whom the beauty of the spring, the glory of the summer, the ripeness of the fall, and the white splendor of winter often come on bootless errands. The reserves mean not mere living, then, but what gives life worth in this simple and natural sense; and we may all cry, who have these empty lamps, to our sorrow,—

> " 'Tis life of which our nerves are scant,
> Life, and not death, for which we pant,
> More life, and fuller still, we want."

II. These reserves mean, in the second place, character; for we can store up character, as we store up life, if we take care and become so rich and strong that, when these sudden and searching emergencies try us as by fire, we suffer no loss, but come out perfect and entire, lacking nothing. For you can all name men of whose stout and sterling manhood you feel so sure that, if one should come to you in the guise of an angel of light, and accuse them of knavery, you would look for the cloven foot on that accuser,— men to whom you could trust your life and fortune and sacred honor, and go to sleep without the least tremor of fear after all the revelations of weakness and wantonness touching great trusts that are enough to wither the heart. They are the men who store up these reserves of character, treasures of insight and foresight, of fortitude and courage, and never lose their head, no matter how the solid earth seems to rock in panic and convulsion, but are strong and quiet, and keep their lamps shining full and clear through the darkness. The trial of their manhood may come, then, when it will, whispering tongues may poison truth, the fearful and unbelieving may desert them, and those even who believe in them most thoroughly may be troubled; but their reserves will not fail. The clear shining from their lamp will not end in a smoke and a stench. They will stand in the evil day; and, when they have done all, stand. The man who has just conduct and character enough to run along in easy times, but lays up no reserves on which he can draw when the cry strikes the midnight of disaster, can have no great peace or joy; but he has both who stores up the reserves on which he can draw when the challenge comes to hold up the light strong and clear.

III. Or these reserves may mean, in the third place, achievement, the power to do the grandest thing possible to our manhood when the demand comes for this reserve, and cube our power out of the latent stores; to do well always, but the best in the crisis on which all things turn; to stand the strain of the long fight with fate or fortune, and still to find we have something left which will meet the uttermost demand.

In our lifetime we shall see no grander instance of this reserve which shines forth in achievement than that Stanley reveals in his story of "Darkest Africa." "In perils of waters, in perils of robbers, in perils of *his* own countrymen, in perils by the heathen, in perils in the wilderness, in perils among false brethren, in weariness and painfulness, in watchings often, in hunger and thirst, in fastings often," to the very clutch of death to cast another black shadow then across the dark continent, the brave heart could not break, the steadfast eyes looked right on, the mighty spirit dominated the weak and failing flesh, the reserves tell the story, the grandest story of these last times.

And so it may be with your life and mine in the things we have to do. We can store up life and light for this crisis of all well-doing when it comes,— an inward and spiritual substance of manhood like that which was found in the great conflict, when delicate, town-bred men would tire down the young giants of the backwoods and prairies, outfight them, and outlive them; and the fine reserves of the Harvard men covered them with glory, while the shallow and brutal might of "Billy Wilson's Regiment" ended in disgrace and shame. An inward and spiritual substance of manhood, I say, nothing can exhaust, which brings us at last to the front with the light burning high and clear from the oil in the vessels with the lamps.

And I have dwelt so long on these more outward truths of the doctrine of the reserves, because they appear to me to be of the utmost worth in this light to those who would come worthily through these tests of our manhood in life, in character, and in the work we have to do; and then, again, because they point inward to deeper and diviner verities we have to mind.

For, as we can store up these virtues against the trial of our outward life, so we can store up other against the trial of our inward life. Faith, hope, and love, and whatever makes the most noble and god-like man as these I have dwelt on, reveal the even man and manhood.

Because, to speak first of our faith in God and his eternal providence and love, we need not merely enough to live through the common experiences of our life, but stores of faith to fall back upon, oil in the vessel with the lamp, when woe and disaster cover our life as with a pall of death. When we wake up suddenly some day to wonder whether God can be in his heaven and we so forlorn on the earth, and if his Christ was not mistaken in his abiding confidence, and the apostles mistaken, and the holy saints, — to wake up with this fear shaking the heart in us, and then to wonder what better we can do than just to grit our teeth and take it as it comes, waiting for the long sleep of death.

Millions of poor, forlorn souls have come to this pass, this *via mala* in the last sore trial of their faith, — the light gone out and no oil in the vessel with the lamp. And I have found in my long ministry many a time that it was of no use trying to give them of my faith, and so try to tide them through, so that they should finish their course with joy. The oil could not pass from man to man,— there seemed to be no channel; and in them there was no reserve. But how many I have found who had struck the same sore troubles, and who were able to rise out of them through the reserves into the very life and light of God! No disaster could overcome them. No trial of their faith could break them quite down. It was no matter that the heavens so neighborly to them of old were black as a starless midnight, save for the pain of it, and the woe, or that "from out waste nature came a cry, and murmurs from the dying sun." The reserves were there. They could say, I know in whom I *have* believed. So they drew on the oil in the vessel with the lamp, and entered into the joy of the Lord.

Poor creatures some of them were, who could give no reason why they should hold on so and stay strong in God, any more than the fountain can give a reason for its flowing, or the plant you find in the desert for the store of cool water in its heart. They also had been sending down roots deep and far, tapping the springs of the reserves, storing up the oil; and then, when the evil day came, nothing could exhaust them of their faith. The old Bible had been drawn on for the reserves, and many another fountain, and, above all, the inward and ever-flowing fountain of God's own life; and, when we do this, there is no peril of the oil giving out. It burns clear and strong unto the eternal life beyond the veil.

Or the still sadder doom may come of shattered hope and a heart like a stone. No haunting any more of the light of a new dawn. No warm pulse toward earth or heaven. Cold ashes only where the fire was, and no more fuel. Dead already, while I still have a name to live. Paralysis in the centres of the soul,— the saddest sight in all the world. The surmise that things can be no worse, and I don't care, just dead hopes, heedless of anything life can give me beyond the dead line. This may come to me when there is no oil in the vessel with the lamp, hopes which rest only on the things which perish in the using, and a love which has never penetrated beyond the senses.

There are no reserves in a life like this to meet the demand. I must still be able to fall back on what is unseen and eternal, or here and now I cannot enter into the light and joy. The men and women you find in this sore strait and stress are of those to whom what we call a good time is the great purpose of their life. But the cry comes, we must all answer, The oil is not forthcoming; and here on the earth is the end. They wist not that these cannot be the final conditions of our faith and hope and love, that there is a soul within the senses to which we must cleave. No reserves are laid up in these shallow, hand-to-mouth ways; and so at last it is as if we heard Azrael, the angel, cry, "Put out the light, and then — put out the light." But the men and women whose faith and hope send down roots into the unseen and eternal, and whose love, while it fills the eyes with light and the ear with music, still loves the vision more than the sight,— and the soul time cannot alter save to make more beautiful, or death touch except to glorify,— these do not turn hard and cold, and say, I will hope and love no more. There is oil in the vessel with the lamp; and heaven and earth may pass away, but the reserves shall not pass away.

But there is still another word. We think of those poor damsels turning away from the closed doors, but still saying, as they go home: We have learned our lesson. We will never be caught again. We will see to the reserves henceforth, and enter with the rest into the light and joy. It is but the suggestion of the way the infinite tender pity and love must open toward hapless human souls left down here in the dark,— the faith we love to cherish who dare, that life is a school in which we learn by failing as well as by succeeding; the faith that no man need sit down in despair even here, and say, That was my last chance, or have those who care for him say, What he was down here he will be forever. I can tolerate no such conception of the love of God. Only this can be true, I say, that our extremity is the divine opportunity, no matter where we are; and, when one door shuts, another opens, is as good an axiom heavenward as it ever can be earthward. We must submit to the sorrow and loss; but we shall learn the lesson, and enter at last into the joy.

The battle-cry of the regiment when they must again face the foe was the name of a fight which had covered them with shame and confusion of face; and, when this new day closed, they had burned out the disgrace, set the smoke of the old shame itself ablaze by their valor, came home with the light burning high and clear, and were met with great sobs of joy by men who thought they had forgotten the secret of tears. And we can all do this, by God's help and blessing, so that no man need despair here; while this is the grander and diviner truth,— that no man will be permitted to despair hereafter, when he has well learned the lesson of the oil in the vessel with the lamp.

INSTANTANEOUS PHOTOGRAPHS.

"As the appearance of a flash of lightning."—EZEKIEL i. 14.

I WENT on an evening, some time ago, to see a great wonder in one of our public halls. It was a collection of photographs taken on the turn of an instant, when we gathered in our city for a centennial celebration. They were flashed for us here against a great white curtain, as you know; and there was a pleasant comment touching each of them in its turn by one of our artists whose words on such themes I always love to hear.

And the object and subject that evening were both well fitted to draw such an audience, if that was all we cared for, to match the pictures on the curtain with those which had caught our eye that day, have them bring all things to our remembrance, and then to wonder whether this flash through which the thing was done can make the shadows abide, so that, when another hundred years have come and gone, those who are living then will be able to gather as we did and see once more the great panorama on land and water which vanished for us in the watching.

To do this, and then to think of the words they will still be reading then, "The fashion of this world passeth away," but still to say, The heavens abide, and the earth and man; to smile at some things they will see, and, it may be, weep at some; to see here and there a face they seem to know, as my old friend saw one in his audience, when he was preaching away out on the prairies in the West,— a face which haunted him through all the sermon as that of a familiar friend who had long ago gone to her rest; to come down when the sermon was over, and say to the woman, If I did not know Mary had been in heaven so many years, I should be ready to believe she was here to-day, and she answered, I am Mary of the third generation,— this was my thought as I sat in the hall that evening, watching the lights and shadows those deft and cunning hands had caught and held for us; but still the greater wonder lay within the passing show. What can be so fleeting as these on the water and in the sky on that April day? They were caught and held in these pictures, never abiding and never returning, just as they were that moment, to endure for a time we have not yet measured. So "who knoweth the way of a ship on the sea?" the ancient wisdom asks; and here was one answer. These ships were caught and held for us, with their flags flying in the wind, with the smoke pouring from their guns, with the sailors on the cross-trees and the citizens on deck. And on the land as on the water here was the same wonder: we were caught and held, as the clouds were in the sky, and the curl on the waves and the spray. The look in your eyes was there, and the turn of your hand on its errand to your comrade, or friend. The remark was on your lips, and the smile on your face, or the frown: only I saw no frown that I remember in the whole succession of the pictures. The foot was arrested tiptoe in the military step where five hundred marched as one. The banners were flying in the wind again, and the shadows chased the lights. The music was in the air: you could almost feel the reverberation, as the deaf do. There it was; and we were there caught and held, to appear on the white curtain while these things endure:—

> "The passing show, the fair spring morn,
> The streets, the trees, the blossomed thorn,—
> These, and far greater things, but caught
> Like these, and to the curtain brought
> The outward semblance made to give
> Enduring life to those that live.
> And, choosing each his moment well,
> Shadow and light their story tell."

Done in a moment, in the twinkling of an eye, there we were,— in our royal youth, in our white age, in our habit as we lived that day, and with the life on our lips and in our eyes. The passing of an instant, and all unawares the picture of a century taken "as the appearance of a flash of lightning."

But I have said the greater wonder to me lay within the passing show, as it opened then and since then, and asked this question, May there not be a good and true lesson for us all in this which was and is now no more save as it is cast against the curtain?—an intimation of the way our lives may be caught in a picture or in a gallery of them, our fellows will bend over in a tender pride or in a sore dismay long after we have done with it all and gone our ways. We walk through this world and life, or stand and gaze, with no more thought of this befalling us than we had that day; take our place in the great procession of life and time each one, and then in a moment the delicate silvered glass is made ready for us in some human spirit, the light flashes on it, the slide goes home, and there we stand. There we stand with the leer in our eyes, or the look in them God's angels love to see; and, with the ban or the benediction on our lips, the very essence of what we are is caught and hidden away, and the work is done. We should make up a face and fall into a posture if we could but be aware of what was coming; but this can never be. This watcher wants the man or woman within all the masks. So he bides his time, takes the picture and hides it away; and then the time may come when it will be cast against the great white curtain, so that all who care to look shall see the real man or woman.

Nor can I think this is some mere freak of my own imagination, when I explore the treasure-trove of such pictures taken through all time, and notice how one swift flash, "as the appearance of a flash of lightning," is about all we have of great numbers; but the flash reveals the man or woman in their *habit*, as they lived and moved and had their being.

In our Bible — the one book in all the world to me which is honest as the day — it is all we have of Enoch, who walked with God. He has no word to say to us, and does nothing save this; but I seem to want no more. The quiet, simple presence rises before me with that light in the eyes and on the face we have all seen in those who walk with God; and so I do not wonder, when the end comes, that it should be no end at all, but *the* beginning rather, as when sunset meets sunrise on the far North Cape on the midsummer night.

So it is again with Lot's wife. She has no word to say to us, and we do not even know her name, while all she does is done in that supreme moment when she grows hard, poor soul, and bitter as the bitumen, what time she cannot tear herself away from her burning home, cannot hear the cries of her children or the imploring of her husband, but must linger by the wreck and ruin; and there in the fatal moment the picture is taken, and there she stands forever with the agony in her eyes, and becomes to the Eastern imagination a pillar of salt.

So the watcher with the glass waits for the prophet again, who beats the dumb beast while it turns its speaking eyes on him in pain and wonder to plead against the cruel strokes. Those eyes speak forever now, and the man sits there forever to point a truth we may all take to our hearts; that even an ass in the right is nobler than a prophet in the wrong, and that is not an easy lesson for the most of us to learn, if I may make the guess.

So the light flashes on Job again as he sits on the ashes of his harried home, and moans out his marvellous monologues of "providence, foreknowledge, will, and fate." There he is forever with the pained and perplexed soul in him laid bare, and somehow we do not care much for him in the years that come before or after: this is the accepted time for the picture. It flashes on Miriam as she stands with her hands lifted, striking the timbrels and singing her grand song of deliverance from the hosts and the sea; and on Deborah, sitting under the palm-tree judging Israel and imparting courage to the captain to deliver the tribes; while Jonah flees from duty to doom, returning from doom to duty to sit under the withered gourd, and be taught of God the great lesson of his loving-kindness and tender mercy to those that know not their right hand from their left.

It flashes frequently on David, who was so many men in one, and so sends down many portraits,—of the shepherd boy on the hills, singing his forever lovely psalm; the young soldier, armed for battle with a stone and a sling; the hapless young husband, robbed of his wife; the king in the presence of the prophet after the great transgression; the heart-broken father mourning for his sons. Many a picture is taken by a flash of David, the shepherd, psalmist, soldier, statesman, sinner, and saint,—the man who could swear like a trooper and praise like a seraph, take vengeance out of the Lord's hands into his own, to see how his curses came down on his own head and his sins turned to serpents by his own hearthstone, to find nothing of any worth at last but penitence for his sin, the infinite pity and love of God, and a manful striving after a better life. Turn where we will in the Bible, we are sure to find our sun pictures gleaming and burning with the life they must reveal. Beautiful or base, it makes no matter to the honest old book and the sensitive silvered glass, while time only brings out into sharper relief the divine or infernal lights and shadows his tooth can do nothing to destroy or mar.

And in the life which draws us nearer home, when

we turn from that little nook of the world, in parable or story, we still find these pictures which reveal the man or woman whole and, as we say, "all there." The light flashes on the matchless old Greek in his prison, rubbing the poor limb from which the fetter has been shorn away, what time he holds high converse with his friends, while the cup he must drink presently to his death stands there on the table,— he sits in the light forever. And on the good Alfred, the Saxon, by his mother's knee, bending in wonder over the beautiful Gospels; in the herdsman's hut, musing over his woe-stricken kingdom while the cakes burn he should have minded, and the good housewife gives him a piece of her mind,— not true, you say: then, I answer, it ought to be, and so *it is*,— Alfred stealing into the camp of the heathen, where those that had desolated his people required of him a song; stealing out again to call his England to arms, restoring peace to the kingdom, establishing the churches, enriching the schools, making his land and ours shine with law and order, with devoutness and scholarship, and then going to his rest. We have many pictures of Alfred: they reveal the manifold man. He wist not it would be so; but the lights were flashing here and yonder that the pictures might be done for all the ages to see, and he did not care. Why should he? Alfred was safe.

And on Bruce, the king, rising from his couch of straw in the barn, when the spider succeeds at the fourteenth trial, to go forth to try again and make his Scotland free at Bannockburn. On John Knox in the presence of the queen and her minions, hurling at them the thunderbolts of his righteous wrath. On Cromwell at Dunbar and Marston Moor, and in the presence of the derelict commons growling, Take that bauble away. On Luther, standing to his answer at Worms, and crying, I cannot do otherwise, so help me God! On Wesley, standing on his father's gravestone to ring out the glad tidings when they had barred the doors of the church. And on Channing, hastening to the Court House in Boston to sit down beside the man they had dragged through the streets of the great free city—the mother city of our freedom—because he would break the yoke of the slave. And on John Brown, staying to kiss the little child as he marches to the gallows with his heart as high as on the day he went to his wedding.

On Mary Ware, the lovely sister of our faith, at Darlington, in Durham, not caring for her errand to see the great motherland, but staying her feet that she might nurse the poor creatures in their fever-stricken homes. And Florence Nightingale, standing before those doors in the Crimea bolted fast with red tape, while the men were dying for food and medicine, and saying quietly, "Bring the axes, and cut down those doors." And on Mother Bickerdyke, we knew so well, in the West, kindling her fires in the roar of the battle to make soup and coffee for "her boys"; and, when one in command said, "Who ordered you to make those fires?" answered, "God Almighty, sir," and went on with her work for the boys, blessing and blest.

There they stand in the wider world and life we know of, never suspecting again the presence of the wonderful silvered glass. Then the slide moves, the light flashes, the thing is done; and the man or woman is taken to stand against the great white curtain of time. Taken for a few years, it may be, or a century, or a millennium, we cannot tell, only that, as in this prophet's vision, the living creatures ran and returned as a flash of lightning; and the rings of the wheels were full of eyes.

And so the truth stands for us, all I would love to tell this morning. These lives of ours, also, are not so much a chronicle, when we reach the heart of the mystery, as a picture or a succession of pictures taken in "a term as brief as the wave's poise before it breaks in foam," and then hidden away in some human heart or memory, so that I shall never suspect this was done to me for honor or shame.

Unaware of it as the lark was Shelley heard singing far up in the heavens; but he sings forever now. He can never be silent until the great and beautiful genius which caught him on the wing has passed away into nothingness and night. Unaware of it as the good parson of a town was, or the poor "wydowe in a poor cottage," standing in a dale, in Chaucer's matchless gallery, there they stand, fresh and fair, after five hundred years have come and gone.

So, indeed, it is true, as the Master says, there is nothing secret which shall not be revealed or hidden which shall not be made known; while these pictures taken of us, as I said, have nothing to do with my posturing or contriving about the way I shall look when I am cast against the white curtain. The living creatures which come and go and flash the lightning take the man unmasked. I may be destined to live in some obscure corner and die there; but, as surely as I live and die, I have stood for my picture,— my picture, which will be noble or base as I am myself, or be blended of both as I am myself, or as he was who sang the great psalms of the ages, so that those who possess the likeness will say, as Father Taylor said of Webster when he was dead, "He was hardly good enough to keep, but too good to throw away." Neither for good nor evil can I live my life and escape the sensitive silvered glass, or, as we hear men say sometimes, cover my tracks. These, in the solemn issues of my life and yours, are like those footprints of the birds caught in the soft mud, it may be, a hundred thousand years ago. The slime hardened into rock, the rock sank and rose again; and now the master restores the bird, they tell me, from the footprint in the rock.

But, in touching this truth, I must not forget another I saw in those pictures that night, as they were cast against the great white curtain. I saw no evil look on any face, so far as I now remember, or "hateful smirk of boundless self-conceit, which seems to take possession of the world, and make of God our tame confederate, purveyor of our appetites." Many of them were anything but comely, and some were ploughed and scarred; but they were at their best and not at their worst, and so I caught the truth on the wing that, while I cannot cheat these watchers, they cannot cheat me and make me seem worse than I am, if I seem no better. So, if there is a real grain of good in me, this is what they have to wait for and watch for, as the mother watches her wayward son, or the wife her husband, or the friend his friend. They wait for the moment when the good overmasters the evil, when the soul of goodness in things evil comes up to breathe: then the light flashes on us as the appearance of a flash of lightning, and we go our ways, unaware of what was done; but the picture is there in their heart, all right. It is the loyalty of heaven and the angels of the burning wheels to the poor grains of worth in the dust and chaff, and I may be winnowed down to that; but there is the tiny store of the good seed of the kingdom, there the bit of real gold within the dross.

It was about all there was in Peter once on a time, and in the woman who wept at His feet who was so good to her and gracious; but the great divine heart in him saw the gold within the dross, and what he saw God sees. So I must not be disheartened or over-fearful that, in the bitter battle between what the apostle calls the law in my members and the law in my mind, I shall have to stand as the evil one, if there is any heart in me of real striving for the divine image and likeness, or that these watchers with the silvered glass are waiting round a corner somewhere to take me at my worst, to flash the light on me then alone, and say, This is the man, or this the woman. In all the world and all time you shall find this to be true, and we can almost say this only: that in our human life, as in other treasures, we love best to find the gold in the dross and shard; and so on this ground also we may gladly believe that the dogma of our total human depravity is a grosser affront to Heaven than it can be to you and me. I would not tamper with the evil things, the sins and shames, God knows, or call black white in their interest. We must hate sin in all its incarnations, and be sure that only fools make a mock at sin. But here is the truth we should always remember: that in God's great garden, which lies outside all the fences we have to make and maintain, that the fairest and best may bloom and ripen, there is not one worthless weed,—*not one.* And so I was glad to hear the low, sweet note of the gospel of nature, shall I say, in the word of a very noble woman, one day, who said she loved to watch the exquisite color, when the spring comes, of what we call a skunk cabbage. There was beauty and grace for her in a thing like that. But all the more is this truth to be taken to heart when we give our heart to all goodness and truth. We may feel sad, then, and weary, and say: What is the use? it is as when wheat is sown on the granite. It is not true the picture is taken strong and clear on the hearts prepared to receive it, and cast in God's good time against the white curtain. We are "children of the light and the day."

Are you standing true to your trust, then, for the nobler picture,—you men and women, you merchants and men of affairs, artists, artisans, teachers, learners, lone men, lone women, mothers in the home, and fathers? Believe me, it is all right. There are galleries of you in the good human heart, taken at your best and all unawares; and what others have you have. It is the holy law of life and of God. Yes, and there may be no word to hearten and inspire you. I cannot be sure about that. Or you may tread the wine-press alone, and another may drink the wine. I do not know about that. But your faith in life, in the truth, in goodness, in God, waits for the true moment; and then, all unawares to us, the glass is ready, the slide shifts silently, and the picture is taken for blessing, when we, as we say so blindly, "are no more." Every true man and woman is so caught and held for the world's diviner life. No such endeavor is only as the shadows which were passing over the waters and the land on that day of the great celebration. Some true word you say, some right, good thing you do, the essence of your very self at your best, is arrested and held as the bright waters were then, and the flying banners, and the sunlight on the presence of the great multitudes. It flashes the true fatherhood and motherhood on the hearts of the children who cannot keep a chronicle, but can only take impressions and pictures; and then, in long years after they are done, they come out and shine on the white curtain in the light that never lay on land or sea, and so never you fear that the picture will be false if the life and love be true. And so may we all believe. The reformer who stands on the first line in the forlorn hope of some truth which will win the world to its banner; the forlorn martyr who cannot die, and yet dies daily; the faithful and true witness whose church counts just one member, and, as he dreams, will die when he dies,— these, and more than I can name in all the world and in all the ages, they stand against the white curtain, not having received the promise, but seeing it afar off. And in all the world and all the ages there they stand also, the watchers with the good silvered glass. The slide is shifted, the light flashes, the picture is taken; and the world and all our life grow more divine and good as we look on them cast against the great white curtain of time. *He* in whom we live and move and have our being has not left us to wonder how the thing will come out; for

> "All things once, are things forever.
> Soul once living lives forever.
> Blame not what is only once,
> When that once endures forever.
> Love once felt, though soon forgot,
> Moulds the heart to good forever."

THE LOW-LYING LIGHTS.

"Let your light so shine before men that they may see your good works, and glorify your Father which is in heaven."—MATT. v. 16.

I. WE may easily see—when we read this Sermon we think of as the sum of all true preaching — that the preacher has no word to say about the church we shall join, the system of doctrine we shall embrace, or the things we shall do that we may think of as essential in ordinance and observance before this light he speaks of can shine forth in and from our life.

And this was by no means because they were all of one mind in old Jewry any more than we are now about such things; for we need not stray outside the Gospels to learn that they had their diverse sects also. There were not so many of them, to be sure,—four perhaps, all told, or five with the Samaritans. Yet he takes no notice here of any sect, but only of the light which may shine from within them, no matter where they may belong.

And, because there were sects among them, these had their systems of belief and of ordinance and usage on which they rested and turned. They were orthodox and liberal, high church and low, conservative and come-outer, with no more aptitude to blend and be one than we have now; but he has no word to say about the need there is to accept this system or that before this light can shine he thinks of as the essential thing to mind. It can shine through them all, if they are sincere and true to the light as the light is to them, or apart from them all, if the light which is in them be darkness.

They had their famous preachers also, and teachers, then as we have now,— the men who had split a prism from the great white shaft of the eternal truth of God, and inserted it for a glass in their souls' windows, through which the light that was in them must shine, dark and lurid or sweet and fair; but he does not say, You shall go to them, and light your lamp there, because it is within them lighted already, in a glimmer or a glory, and what they have to do is to let it shine.

They were very simple folk, also, he had about him, in the main,— poor men, of a very limited education and attainment; and, if he had asked them what they believed and why, they would most likely have stammered and blundered, and got the statement twisted all out of true on their uncouth and rustic tongues the moment they strayed beyond the things they had learned by rote in the school and synagogue.

Yes; and very likely would have mixed up the Bible truth with some of the common currency, just as such a man quoted the words from the Bible to me a good many years ago, "God tempers the wind to the shorn lamb," and, when I said, That is not in the Bible, ruminated for a while, and then answered, "Well, if it isn't, it ought to be," and to that I said, Amen.

It is well worth our while to notice also that this

gracious monition was given to men, and no doubt to women, too, who would be so full of care about their day's work of some sort, and their daily bread, that beyond the simple faith which would lie within the life they were living, and the work they were doing on the land and water and in their homes, there would be no light in them save this, perhaps: that they must do as they would be done by, and fall back, for the rest, on some such heart of grace as that we find in good Dolly Winthrop in the story,—"Ah! there's a deal o' trouble in this world, Master Marner, and things we can never make out the rights on; and all we can do, then, is to trust,—to do the right thing so far as we know, and to trust. For, if us as knows so little can see a bit o' good and right, we may be sure there's a good and a bigger rights nor what we can know. And it's the will o' Them above as many things should be dark to us; but there's some things as I've never felt i' the dark about, and they're mostly what comes i' the day's work." So they must think of what they had to do in this world, and put their life into that day by day and all the year round, or they could not keep the home together, and pay their way like honest men and good women.

And, in doing this, who should know better than he did who was talking with them, and had lived in a home like theirs all his life, what a hard struggle it would be not seldom to make ends meet, and drive the wolf from the door in those evil and desperate times? How the light which was in them would be darkened by clouds of fear, when the harvest was scant and poor, and the lord of the land ruthless for his rent, when sickness invaded the home, and it grew dark in the shadows of death, when the fishing was naught on the Sea of Galilee, or the boat lay a wreck on the beach with the father and sons down within the wild waters, while the widow and children that were left wept for the sore desolation! This he knew because he knew what was in man and a man's life, and because he had lived in the heart of it for thirty years, and had seen the pathetic sight he touches in a parable, where the poor house-mother finds her sixpence lost in the mud floor, and rushes out, crying to the neighbors and friends, "Rejoice with me, for I have found the piece which was lost." All this he knew,— the preacher with the divine heart and the light in it which has grown to be the glory of the world. Yet he said to them, Let *your* light so shine before men that they may glorify your Father which is in heaven. And so this light, if we have caught his meaning, is not of a sect or system or a say-so of any sort. It is there by the ordination of God, striving to shine forth through the thick encrustations that overlay the soul's windows, or shining strong and clear from clean and strong souls; but, whatever may be the estate of the glass, there is the light, and they must let it shine.

II. And so it is once more that when, for my soul's sake, I read this word of the Master as it stands, clear from the conditions we make for the shining now,— that we shall believe this or that, as it is set forth in the diverse books, and do this or that we are bidden to do, or the light which is in us will be not light, but darkness,— I still hear the voice of Him who spake as never man spake beside, saying: Let not your heart be troubled about these contentions, over "This is the false" and "That is the true," which vexed the world in my time as it vexes the world in yours. There is the light within you which was within me, — the light which cometh down from heaven. Now let it shine. It may be hard for you to keep the glass clear always, — mine was not clear always, — but mind the light. And there may be those who will say of you what they said of me, — that your light is not from heaven, but from the pit. Let them say what they will, let it shine. This is what you are here for, — to reveal the light which is in you; and you may think it is of no use and no one cares, while there are always those who love the darkness rather than the light, and they may hate you for the shining as they hated me. But you must be true to the shining all the same.

The argument which goes right home to the heart where all words fail is the argument of the light shining clear through the windows of sincere and true souls, — yours or mine, — when we keep the glass sweet and fair. Then, as I listen again, I see that gracious look my holy preacher casts on those who hear him, and still note the emphasis he hides in the words "let *your* light shine"; and then it is as if he had said to them what he would say to us also. You will go home from hearing this word of mine to your fishing and farming, your vines and olives, and flocks of sheep, or your business in the town over yonder; and for the most of you this is all you can do, or ever will do, while you live on the earth. And now the truth I would tell you is this: that you can let your light so shine there on the land or the water, in your homes and in the business you have to mind, that you may live and pay your way, like honest men and true, and good women and true,— so shine that there shall be a divine worth in it for the world you live in and for all time to come; and then the word shall be said to you when your work is done: "Well done, thou good and faithful servant! enter thou into the joy of thy Lord." Very little you may be able to do, as you think of it, beyond what you must take hold of to-morrow, and the kindly and neighborly service, also, which comes with the day by day. But this world and your life, these are in our Father's hands as surely as the innermost and the uttermost heavens are; and you serve him then as surely as the angels of the presence which stand about the throne. Therefore, all things whatsoever ye would that men should do unto you, do ye even so unto them. This is the law and the prophets. And if ye, being evil, know how to give good gifts unto your children, how much more shall your Father in heaven give good things to them that ask him!— this is your faith. And behold the fowls of the air, who sow not, nor reap, nor gather into barns, yet your heavenly Father feedeth them; while not a sparrow falleth to the ground without his will, and ye are more than many sparrows,— this is your trust. And blessed are the lowly of heart, and blessed those that mourn, and blessed the meek, and blessed the merciful, and blessed the pure in heart, for they shall see God,— these are your beatitudes. And a good tree cannot bear evil fruit,— this is your evidence. And now go home, and let your light so shine before men.

III. So I have lingered over this great and most pregnant monition of the Master, as I said, because it stands good for all time and comes home to us all. Down on the coast, this summer, I was watching a light from my window, when, as the word runs in my mother land, it was blowing great guns. It was not a great light, like the Minot on that coast and that on Sandy Hook our way, but a hand fed the lamp we never see and always see,— the hand of the republic and the day's man of the republic was within the small, sturdy tower. And, as the sun went down, the light flashed out; and at midnight, as I turned away from the window, there was the light shining clear over the dark waters. Then I said, This is not something for the man in the tower there to talk about, but something to do,— to stand true to the light; while to let it go out or burn down dim, when the order is to keep it burning strong and clear, would be to lose his rank, and number as one who had proven unfaithful to his trust.

And so I got a parable out of it all, touching this gracious monition in the Master's sermon, and how we must all mind the light, not in another's way, but in our own, as the day's men of God; while it will be a good day for the world, a quaint old divine says, when we once come to the conclusion that God cares a great deal more for the clear shining than he cares for what we say about ours being the finest and the best. And then is it only a low light *we* have to mind, not a splendid glory like those we have all seen. So was that in the sturdy little tower on the coast; but the man who had to mind it was as true to his calling and election as the day's man of the republic, as those are in the high places, and as they were on Cape Race, whose light on a black midnight, **twenty years** ago, warned us away from the fatal shore. Indeed, I find that the men and women who are dearest to me, as the years grow from the few to the many, are not those who challenge the world to admire and praise them, but rather those who have stood faithful to the low-lying light, as the man whose lamp I was watching is to those who live about the Bay which lay beyond my window, and who have to look to him for help and direction when the need grows sore.

And so, as I think of these faithful in a very little, one comes out from the mist and silence of the years who has moved on these many years to the land where there is no more night and no more sea. He was in my old mother church, and always said one prayer, and told one very simple story, with very much endeavor to get it out, about what lay in his heart, while we all knew it word for word before he began. And, then, no matter who was the preacher, he would go quietly to sleep, as a child will, the moment we gave out our text, and sleep right through the sermon; while even in the prayer-meetings, when the rest were very wide-awake indeed, he would go to sleep, and wake up now and then to say Amen. But, if in all the world he could have found an enemy,— a thing you could not imagine, — he could not have got one other man to believe that old George was not sincere and true as the saints of God are; while he was the one man everybody ran to in their troubles, and would be likely, as they ran, to meet him half-way, coming to look them up and help them. He was not a rich man; but his hand and heart were always open, and his time seemed to belong to all the folk within hail of his home. Managing small estates for widows and orphans; the president of the temperance cause in the valley, where in the meeting the speech he never did quite make touched you more potently, when you knew the man, than the choicest eloquence of other men ; and the wildest fellows in the shops would be ready to sign any pledge when he would look at them out of his soft brown eyes, and plead with them that they should quit drinking with such a tender pathos that they would break into tears and swear mighty oaths they would drink no more, and then ask him to forgive the swearing. And George had a pony he had raised himself and trained, so resolute to have his own way, and stop when it pleased him, that the president of the society down the street would have told him, I think, to try the whip. Ah! but the light shone so clear in the good old heart and life, and he stood by it so loyally through the eighty years, hearing and heeding the monition to keep the glass clear, and mind the light in the low-standing tower. In his work on the farm and his worship in the old meeting-house, his visitings of the fatherless and the widows in their affliction, his oversight of whatsoever things were true and lovely and of a good report, and his good hospitable heart, and merciful and tender, this was how the light shone for us all, and made good the divine monition.

IV. So, as I read the words again and think of the light I saw in the summer athwart the Bay, I can see how the truth opens we may all take to our hearts about the low-lying light.

It may shine, first of all, on the work we have to do in this world, where we are all coworkers together with

God on this work; and when from it, when we create and do not destroy true wealth and worth, as workmen who need not to be ashamed. In the bonnie greenlands I love to find where I may, far from this busy city, there is not the least need, I notice, for me to sit down with the husbandmen, and ask them what light they can shed on fair and true farming: the light lies on the farms, or the shadows, wherever I go. On the grass in the meadows, and the growing corn; on the trees in the orchards and the flowers in the door-yard the mother and daughters tend, and on the sweet and simple homesteads,— on these the light tells the story, and on those where the light is darkness, and must struggle through the glass encrusted by sloth or worse, set forth in the squalor and neglect. It is the simplest truth we can take to our hearts when we begin where the Master began for proof and evidence in the low-lying light. It shines on the farm and the workshop, and on all we have to do, no matter how near it may lie to the base line of our life, and no matter how high it may reach toward the stars; and here men may see our good works, and glorify our Father which is in heaven. So is it hand work? Very well. Or work the world calls noble? Very well. Or humble? Very well. The day's work of the carpenter's son, Cyprian reports, at ox yokes and ploughs? Very well. Or this Sermon on the Mount? Still very well. Here is the law and the testimony he made good in his own life, that we shall mind the light where our life lies and our work in this world.

And, again, we shall do this for our own sakes, because, as the hand we never see and always see clasps the oil, the glass, and the flame the man must mind in that low-lying light-house on the coast, or he loses his rank and number, so we must let our light shine, God's hand clasps lest we lose ours. And, as the man ordained by the Republic to mind the light can never quite tell what worth lies in the clear shining, no more can we, save by faith in his faithful endeavor and as we stand true to this trust.

If my dear old friend could have dreamed that forty years and more from the time we first met I should pay my poor tribute to the low-lying light which shone for us to the end of the years, he would have said: What am I doing worth a moment's mention or memory? I cannot help it, there is no merit in it: I am only doing that which it is my duty to do. But I must have answered, Old friend, you are seeing to the lamp and keeping the glass clean and fair, you are standing true to the light; and it is not for you to know what worth lies in your steadfastness and truth.

> "Lives of great men all remind us
> *We* can make our lives sublime."

It is not for us a question of greatness, but of faithfulness to the Master's word.

So I have read of one who was left alone in some tower with a flashing light where the machinery broke down, and the darkness came on, and the storm. Then he saw what he must do: he must contrive some rude purchase which would still flash the light. And there he stood all night, turning the thing at such cost that, when the relief came in the morning, he had fallen down, done almost to death with the terrible strain. But, when they asked him how he could do it,— this work which would be heavy for two strong men,—he answered, "I thought of them out there in the storm and darkness looking toward my light, and how they would need it to save them; and then I knew I must mind the light, live or die. So I cried, 'God help me to help them out yonder,' and stood to it until the day broke and the sun came up out of the sea." And so I stand here to tell you the best I know; but it is only as when one playeth upon an instrument some pleasant or sad tune, if I have to say, with a poor old man I heard of, Mind the light, and let the lantern go, when the lantern and the light are each essential, — the man and the word. Are you in the store, then, or the workshop, the market or on the farm, in the home, in the study, in the studio, in the school? Is it a poem through which the light will shine, a picture, a book, a lesson, an invention, a ledger, a wagon-wheel, a horse well shod, a stone wall, a business that touches both the poles, everything, anything which creates and does not waste and destroy? Labor is prayer. The light shines in and from what we do, when the loyal heart is in it, and the faithful hand; and the Lord and Master only set his seal on the divine sermon as it stands in the Gospels for all men to read, because he made the truth he tells, and the light that shines in and through it all on the noblest and best we can be and do, real to us, and true as the way, the truth, and the life. Or do we say, finally, I am of this sect or the other, a follower of Fox, the apostle of this inward light, or Wesley or Channing? Well enough, I answer; but, if that is all, you are only a reflector of another man's light, and, good as this may be, it is not the best.

The best for you is yours, the best for me is mine, if I look to the lamp, and keep clean and fair the glass. This light which shone so strong and clear from the Master's heart as he sat on the hillside, and still shines so strong and clear, came to him from the fountain of light, the Father of lights, the primal source, the sun which lights the suns and tips the glow-worm with its lambent lamp, and thence comes our light, or should come; and we only follow him truly herein when we follow him to the fountain, the Father, the eternal, immortal, and invisible, who is light, and in him is no darkness at all. Amen.

THE CITY LIETH FOUR-SQUARE.

"The city lieth four-square, and the length is as large as the breadth. The length and the breadth and the height are equal."— REV. xxi. 16.

IT was the holy city the seer saw coming down out of heaven from God, where the noble should dwell, and gentle, the clean and true; and these should come from the east and west, the north and south, and enter within the gates, which stand open always for their welcome. And the city had no need of the sun, for the glory of God did lighten it; and standeth four-square, and her gates open every way, and he foretells how the nations shall walk in the light of it, and the kings of the earth shall bring their glory and honor into it. It is a vision of the commonwealth of God he sees through the lurid smoke and flame, where we may all dwell who are of this heart and mind, no matter whence we come, what may be our name, or from what direction we may come,— east or west, north or south. If this is what we bring with us,— nobleness and gentleness, sincerity and truth of the heart and purpose,— we can enter, then, and sit down together in the heavenly place, and be citizens of the commonwealth of God.

But, as I muse over the vision so large and fair and

all-enfolding, I have to wonder how many of us dwell there now, or are near indeed to the ever-open gates, as I notice how we still stand aloof, and call each other names not seldom that sting and burn, because those who cannot think as we do have come from some other direction toward the holy city, and are not one with us in opinion or usage. It makes no great matter, then, how true they may be, and sincere. They are still of one brand, while we are of another; and so it is hard for us even to imagine that their claim can be as good as ours to be fellow-citizens with the saints. They must come on the same line as this we take, and be able to give about the same account of their journey, or else they must be counted of a poorer quality, as in the markets they grade their wheat as one, two, and three; so those of us who count ourselves number one feel we must not be mixed up with two and three, or the whole worth of what we stand for will come into peril. We must keep up the standard; and we mean by this the beliefs and usages which are most nearly like our own, with only a slight regard for the large and fair lines of this noble vision. Not to be of our "domination," as a good woman in Kansas called her sect once, when we talked of these things, is to take a lower place in these questions of the outlook and insight of the soul touching the holy city; and none of us are free from this feeling, or, it may be, can be free. You can find it among the Baptists, where my dear mother belonged, and the Methodists, where I belonged long ago, among the Unitarians, and in the High Church and the Low;

while your Quaker nourishes the feeling as surely as your Catholic that the true way is this we take toward the city of God, and the true side is this on which we enter.

But now is not this true, first of all, that, when we turn from the faith we hold under many names to the life we share as citizens of the republic, we manage to do a good deal better than this by those who come here to seek their fortunes and make their home? These come to us from far and wide, and about all we care for is that they shall be good men and good citizens. They may come from the east, then, with its history, or from the west, with its prophecy, from the hard-headed north or the warm-hearted south; but, if they will only take hold of the work which is waiting to be done in a good and manful way, we are quite content to give them a good welcome. You who are of the old strain may be a little clannish, to be sure, and I think you are; but you do not let this bar the way finally to the wider and more gracious outflow of your life, and you may count us who are new-comers back to our race and nation, while as yet you know very little else about us, because this is one way, and on the whole a very good way, to find the lines at once of our worth and our limitations. Still, this is swept aside handsomely and well when you are once sure of your man, and find, as we say, that he is all there, and means to be. He may come from any direction; but you count this of no great moment in the exact measure of the deepness and worth of your insight, and think it is a shame to discount his claim by saying,

Ah! but he is an Englishman, or an Irishman, or a German. If he is a good sterling *man*, one who weighs well in the scales of honesty, usefulness, and virtue, you are quite content to count him in; and, then, I notice that those who are of the old stock are ready to make ample amends for any touch of hesitation they may have felt in giving such a one the right hand of fellowship while as yet he was an unknown and untried man.*

You may notice once more that, when we strike still wider lines than these, we are able to see where the worth lies of this greater and fairer judgment, and in a still finer light. This was one of the lessons, I remember, which came to me in our great centennial year, and also when I went to the Exposition in Paris two years after, in 1878. There, in each instance, were the noblest arts and inventions of the nations, east, west, north, and south, set forth in their best estate; and they all had this worth in them of the manhood which looks backward or forward, of the warm and fluent nature, or of that which works to severe and hard lines.

So in the best work of the old eastern lands you could easily trace the worth of tradition and reflection and the spirit which goes backward, while in the best work of the western there were enterprise and anticipation and the spirit which looks forward. And strong and stern work came from the north; while from the south came the most wonderful exuberance in form and color and a plastic softness, touched here

---

* A'ways except when he is a Chinaman, and this is to our shame.

and there with a half-savage energy or a seductive underplay of fancy, which was just the reflex of the manhood which gave us the treasure. It was to be seen in all the fabrics and pictures that were genuine transcripts of each land and race. Turn where you would, this was the waiting truth; and, then, it was not hard to see how a completeness of beauty and worth lay within the whole treasure you would have looked for in vain, had any been left out. Take away reflection or anticipation, austerity or emotion, and you could have had no such wonders of worth and beauty either in the finer or the homelier arts. East, west, north, and south were all needed for this revelation which came to us of the best the nations can do; and so the city of God in the arts, I said, as I saw the wonder, lieth four-square, and her gates open every way.

It is the truth again touching the treasure we find in noble books and in all the tracks of the spirit they reveal. Measure these by large and fair lines, and you find we still have to go eastward for the past and westward for the future, northward for cool reason and southward for fervid emotion; that science belongs to our western lands,— the promise of the future,— and the old sacred books to the eastern,— the treasures of the past,— while poetry and music were born of the southern heart, and pure reason and logic of the north.

It is true, to be sure, that these qualities may mix and mingle in the greatest books, as indeed they do, so that there seems to be a confusion in them, like that we notice in the isothermal lines, and the winds which blow where they list to chill you to the bone in Florida when we are fainting with the heat in New York, or to give you a calm in the very temple of the winds and a cyclone in the heart of all stillness. The spirit which is hidden in great books, or shall we say in the greatest, cannot be bound as it may be in other ways. So your supreme books are hard and stern or soft and fluent, and dip backward or forward on grand, free lines of their own. Still, we have only to imagine a world full of books in which there was only one of these treasures to the exclusion of all the rest, no sacred treasures from the past or splendid hopes for the future, no cool reason or glowing emotion, to see how poor we should be where we are now so rich. They are all needed for the revelation of human genius in this spiritual body we call a book. The treasures of the past and the future must be in them, and words that kindle and words that cool. So the city of God in the human heart and intellect also lieth four-square, and her gates open every way. And as it is with the book, so it is with the man who speaks to us by this holy spirit, this *whole* spirit; for, wherever you find such a man, you find the incarnation of these diverse powers and gifts and this grace. So Isaiah and all the greater prophets find their full expression not in prophecy alone, but in reflection also; while they lay stout bolts of reason in the moulds into which they pour the molten gold of their fervid emotion. So Milton must have a "Paradise Lost" before he can afford us a "Paradise Regained," and argue of "providence, foreknowledge, will, and fate" between the lovely interludes of the garden and the first human pair.

This is the secret also of your true orator on the platform or at the bar, in the Senate or the pulpit; and we are all at fault as we lack the power to look backward or forward, to bind our work well together with reason and logic, and to penetrate it through and through, when the demand is there, with the fires of a fervent emotion. Prophecies and Psalms, sermons on Mars' Hill or on Murray Hill, orations that mark an era, or lyceum talks of a man like Tyndall,— scan them all, and you will find these treasures in them in the precise measure of their perfection,— wealthy in anticipation as in reflection, bound well together by reason and logic, and threaded through and through with quick emotion; for this city also lieth four-square, and the length and the breadth and the height of it are equal.

And now would it not be of all things strange to find that this law was of no great moment in the things which touch the soul's life, in religion, which is of such high worth in our whole life besides, or that the main worth in religion should lie in one of these, to the dwarfing and starving of all the rest? Because it is not hard to see how this is no mere notion of mine, but a revelation rather of the way the Most High takes with us to bring out all our powers, each holding its own secret of worth for us, and taking its own place in the perfection I would try to find. And is it not fair, therefore, that we should take this to be the truth about the religious life also, and so venture on the presumption, if we can do no more just now, that, as we can count each of these treasures at their true worth, making none of them supreme over all the rest, but of an equal and beautiful worth all round, we shall find the conditions here of the truest faith and life,—a faith and life in which the priceless treasures of the past will be as dear to us as the most splendid promise of the future, and what holy men of old have said as what holy men say now or will say while the world stands right from the fountains of the divine inspiration, while the processes of reason and logic by which we come to the truth of God shall by no means override the swift intuition which catches a truth on the wing? And may not this revelation of the fourfold treasure help us to the stout and steadfast denial of the claims we are all so ready to make that some one of these treasures is really supreme in its worth, or, if not quite supreme, still of a worth which overshadows all the rest? For myself, I think it is a limitation no church or sect or man need be proud of, any more than we are proud of a limited vision or of color-blindness; and so, when we say that the church which cleaves only to the past, to the sacred books and the traditions and usages which have grown sacred with time, is the only true church, and we want no more and will seek no farther, it seems to me that the only answer to such a claim must be, This is all very good as far as it goes, but it only goes eastward, after all.

Or I may say, I will believe in nothing I cannot reason out to the last word and accent. Well, I can find a very noble treasure of truth in this way also, and feel sure of my ground, as far as it goes; but, then, I may be in peril of the rebuke Dr. Parr made to one who said to him, "Sir, I will believe nothing I cannot understand." "Then, sir," the old man answered, when he had heard him out, "your creed will be about the briefest I ever heard of in all my life." Or there may be no danger of such a rebuke, and no reason for it. Yet, in this wonder and mystery of our human life, by cleaving to my reason and logic, and this alone, I may become the man Wordsworth had in his mind as

> "One to whose smooth, rubbed soul can cling
> No form or feeling, great or small,
> A reasoning, self-sufficing thing,
> An intellectual all in all."

And I do not come, then, toward the city of God. I wander away toward the polar wastes of the soul's divinest life. Or, again, I may give myself over to an intense and overmastering emotion, in which reason has no place, and make the past and future of no account save as food for my fever. Well, this fervid emotion has also a grand story to tell of our human life and history. It has set the world afire time and again, and burned up the dead brakes and timbers to make clear spaces for the new springtime of God. Still, emotion is only of the southward, at the best; and, when I have this, and nothing more, the chances are that I may burn myself up in my burning. And then the pity of it is that in the most of us there is not timber enough to make much of a fire.

Do I dream again over the untold promise of the

future? God forbid that I should cry this down, this vision of new heavens and a new earth; but what is it, after all, but the westward outlook of the city of God? Very good, I know, and quite essential in the wholeness of the treasure,— but that, and no more. For we have all known those who could find no good eastward or north or south of the city, who derided the old sacred treasures, who could not or would not reason, and kept themselves far away from the moving emotions which make the soul's life so fluent and full of grace; but they were rather apt to be of all men wanting, when you needed men to stand by the things which must be done here and now, or their own dream of the future, grand and great as it may be, can never come true. Such men hold true treasure for us all; but, when they care for the westward outlook alone, to the slaying of the rest, they may only be like the outermost pioneers we hear of, who want always to push farther on when the smoke of another chimney shoots a blue thread against the far horizon. They can unite with no society in this commonwealth of God: they can only be content with the wilderness; while, if they could but touch this completeness of the city which lieth four-square, they might still nourish the westward look, and leave the world their debtor.

It must be true, then, and no mere notion of mine, that no one of these grand factors in religion can ever be so true and good for us as the whole. The past holds its high worth with the future: reason is as the iron bolt, and emotion as the fluent life which flows

and flames all about it; and, when we take this truth to
our hearts, we can see how, in this commonwealth of
the religious life, the tendency to take sides and pre-
fer this that or the other is all right so long as we
hold ourselves modestly,— as so many do, thank God,
after all,— and find in it the motive power of the love
which never faileth. Make this law as true in the
commonwealth the seer saw as it is in the world's
great commonwealth, and then it is not hard to see
how the past holds its treasure for us all on one side,
and the future opens its promise on another, how rea-
son here may reign supreme in us, and there a holy
and fervid emotion. So, while we trust we may grow
evermore alike, we can be glad and proud, then, for
the worth which flows from our unlikeness. And still,
allowing that this is the best we can do for ourselves
or, with our nature, the holy spirit of truth can do for
us,— I speak as a man,— we can challenge each other
to bring forth the finest fruit of our diverse endow-
ments, and then match them in no narrow or selfish
fashion, but that the Father may be glorified in all
his sons and daughters. While we who may call our-
selves liberal Christians can only be worthy the name
as we are able to understand this diversity among
sincere men and women of every name in the church
of the living God we accept in nations and races and
in the commonwealth of the arts and the intellect.
So, while we may have to allow that three in the four
sides may not be of our make or mind, yet in the city
of God they all face true.

Has my brother, then, the faith which looks eastward, is the past of supreme worth to him, the sacred books, the saintly lives, the great traditions, the old and deep roots of the life of God in man? Let me be proud of him, then, and glad for him; for he may find treasure there I fail to find, and sit down with the patriarchs and the prophets in their kingdom. Does he look with those gleaming eyes only toward the future trying to see the things not seen as yet, and does he hide his manhood in his peering, does he live for the future, and try to make his vision good here and now? I say, in this way also, he is a citizen of the commonwealth of God; and the men of the westward heart and outlook find all the new worlds. Is he the man who will only reason and draw the truth in this way from the ever-flowing fountains of the life of God? Then woe is me again, if I fail to believe he dwelleth in God, and God in him. He is a worker in the iron of this kingdom. You will find his forge close by the northern gates; and, indeed, we need his bolts and bars always, and never more than now.

Does he dwell by the southern gates of the city, as a man who could not reason if he would, and would not if he could, but counts his fervid emotions of more worth than all besides? Well, I want to know if his emotions are set on fire of heaven, as Melville said of his good comrade, John Knox. Do they burn with a clear flame to all divine ends and issues? We need such men always, and women to match them, in the city of God. They hold the secret in their hearts of the grand and true revivals which wait always for their advent, and preach sermons and pour out prayers over which we wonder after they are dead and gone, and say, Where lay the secret of their power to do such things? They seem now to be so dead; but we might as well wonder over the white ashes of good sound hickory. The substance was burned in their burning, but the world was melted in the fervent fires.

So the truth stands of the solidarity — shall we say? — of the city which standeth four-square, in which

> " All are needed by each one;
> Nothing is fair or good alone."

It is the truth about the commonwealth of God and the city. In that wonder I mentioned, I met a good old man I had known many years, and a Methodist when I was one, who never went to sleep under my preaching; and so I loved him. But, when I left my old mother church, a film came down between our lives and long-enduring love, so that we could see no longer eye to eye. Seventeen years had passed, and here I found him where, for the first time since we parted, he greeted me like a brother. Would I let him show me the treasures in the great halls, and would I eat bread with him? The old life began to beat again, and we went wandering through the wonderworld like two brothers. He was glad and proud for the whole wealth which had come from everywhere,— east, west, north, and south,— and saw how each was unique, and yet part and parcel of the splendid completeness. Then we had a talk about the old times; and I found the good old heart in him had grown greater and more gracious, and he had learned something of the truth the Master touches in his saying, "The children of this generation are wiser than the children of light." Here was a gospel for the commonwealth of God from the commonwealth of man. He was prepared to see what we may do in the divine life in his joy over what had been done in the human, when the suggestion was made that in this, also, we should match the best with the best all round, and be glad for it all, and proud of it all, no matter what may be the brand or whence it may come,— glad for all truth-seekers and all truth-tellers, all the sincere, the noble, the gentle, and the faithful, and the treasures of the old and the hope of the new; and so, when we parted, we were closer together than we had ever been before in one Lord, one faith, and one baptism. And so it may be, and must be, finally. We hear the cry going forth far and wide that not creed, but character, is the standard by which men must be weighed and measured in the good time coming; and then, if we must have our diverse modes of faith and worship, the question for all the churches to answer will be, What sort of men do you raise in there, and women, — noble or mean, sweet or bitter, full of charity or stricken with bigotry, Christ-like and God-like, and loving the light or of those who hug the darkness, and have no part or lot in the city which standeth four-square; and so, in a word, if you ask me,

"What is religion? I will tell you what
I think it is,— not blindly to disdain
Thy reason, or to lay thee flat

Before a something terrible, unknown,
Not bound with bristling fence of man-made creeds
To thunder banns from thy presumptuous throne,
Or bring God down and make his will thine own,
But in his face with reverent love to look,
Here where it shines in sky and land and sea,
And, where a prophet speaks in holy book,
To hear his word, and take that truth to thee,
And hold it fast, and tread earth's lowly sod
With open heart, as one who walks with God."

ANTIPAS, MY FAITHFUL MARTYR.

"Antipas, my faithful martyr."—REV. ii. 13.

THIS is only one brief line about this man, but it stands for a life and a death. We do not know *who* the man was, only *what* he was, a martyr for God and his truth. And there is no word to tell us whether he was a young man or an old man, or had a wife and children or lived his own lone life, or loved this fair world with the love of the morning tide or had got a little tired of it all and was ready to go, or whether he went brave and defiant to his death or shrank back when the great moment came, while the flesh cried "Recant" and the spirit spurred him on.

"Antipas, my faithful martyr," is all they tell us about him; and even this seems to float over to us from the heart of the great Divine Mystery. "I was in the spirit on the Lord's Day," the seer says, "and fell on a vision and heard a voice, and saw, as it were, the Son of Man, and was bidden to write this word, Antipas, my faithful martyr." So this is the way the light flashes for us across the darkness. A person of no account, so far as anybody knows, puts his life in pawn for this faith which had made him a new man; but they will not hurt him, I presume, if he will hold his tongue about it even now, and go with the crowd to the temple, toss a few grains of incense on the fire, and crook his knee. But, if he persists in this fooling, they will have his life; for they have made up their minds to stamp this thing out, and then there is no way open to Antipas but to die.

He had, no doubt, dreamed also, as they all did then, that he might see the heavens open and the hosts of angels sweep down through the azure vault with a great shout, and the dead rise from their graves, and the grand new day of God begin. But there is no hope now that he will ever live to see the day; and so he dies and they have seen the end of Antipas. If they beheaded him, some pious souls might see to the funeral, weeping the while, collect the handful of ashes, and hide them somewhere in a little urn, and then, it may be, scratch a dove or a cross on the cover; and, if they threw him to the wild beasts, there would be a speedier end. "There is an end, anyhow," they said who saw him vanish on that dim forgotten day. "No more trouble about Antipas: he is blotted out." "Yes, out of your books," the Spirit says, "but not out of mine. I have not done with Antipas, my faithful martyr. I will touch his name with one gleam of immortal glory, and make it shine like a star when your names are forgotten. I want this man for a type: he shall stand for the instance of those who die for me and mine, and seem to be forgotten. It is not an end they have made, but a beginning, and not the night which has touched them, but the great morning of God."

Such is the meaning, as it seems to me, of this line which stands for a life and a death; and the truth it tells us is this: that those who stand steady and true to what they believe to be God's clear truth in this world and their own clear duty, and die for it as they have lived, and prompt us to say as we watch them vanish, "How soon we are forgotten!" are never forgotten. There may not be this one line even to tell us how they fought and fell, but this makes no matter. They have passed through a divine alchemy which has transformed the carbon into a gem.

Still, no greater mistake can be made than that we make so often of thinking that your martyrs are only those who live and die for their doctrines and dogmas, though these be never so noble and true. Nor is it unfair to say that a good many of those who, in any age, stand ready to die in such quarrels, would still be no true martyrs if you should put them to death. Some are simply bigots, who, in the days that are gone, would just as easily put those to death who did not agree with them as they would die themselves, and always did this when they had the power. So these could not be martyrs in the high, sweet spirit of Antipas; while others again have stood ready to die, or have died, through a superb egotism or a devouring vanity rather than a quiet and sacred conviction of truth and duty, and gone posturing out of life, feeling that this was the way to immortal glory, and cheap at the price.

Nor can we doubt that, while there is still a true doctrine men may well die for, such doctrines did not mean to men like Antipas what they may easily mean to you and me. They were not an end, then, but a means, and did not settle these questions of the Eternal Life, but started them, rather, and were not so much a specific for the cure of souls as a light on the way towards such a cure, faith that it could be done, courage to denounce the shams and quackeries all about them, and heroism to fight them to the death. So, in the work Antipas was called to do, the death he must die was but the close of the great heroic chapter; and a man like Paul would have been a martyr all the same if he had died in his bed.

We have to notice, also, that the spirit of the age will not allow a man to be put to death for his opinions any more unless he tries to drive them home with lead and steel, so that even old John Brown was not a martyr so much as the last of the Ironsides, who fought on the stricken field, and then, when the battle went against him, slipped out of the body to God. And so it is not only true that a man may die for what he calls his faith, yet be no martyr after all, but this is true, also, that the old paths to the martyr's death by cross and stake are closed; and so it would be no use looking for men to match Antipas if this was the one way to martyrdom. But we know this is not the one way, nor are all the martyrs dead, while the terms on which they live and die are stern as ever, only they take other forms and work to other issues, while that which makes them and the stuff out of which they are made is here; and martyrs die every day, unnoted, easily forgotten, steady as Milton's angels, true as the old saints,—martyrs to truth and duty still and to God and his Christ.

Shall I note some of these? Here is a man who is haunted all his life by some great invention or some supreme discovery in science or the arts a hundred years before the world is ready for it or it can be born from the womb of time; and so he works for this, starves for it, and is a fool over it in the world's common judgment, while still the thing fills him with its bitter-sweet torment. And so he has to die, not having received the promise, but seeing it afar off; and then, when he is dead, if he has any friends left, they draw a long breath, and brighten up a little as they return from his funeral, and say: "Poor fellow, he might have done something very good in the world but for that maggot in his brain. He had splendid powers. What a pity he should throw them all away over such a delusion as that which haunted him so long!"

One such man I knew. He was haunted all his life by the idea of a grander and fairer social order, a new harmony among men, in which the sore conflict between class and class would come to an end, and we would all be brothers. He used to come to see me now and then, and talk it over,—a man with a grand, craggy head and far-looking, deep gray eyes, the eyes of a prophet of the Lord, while it was wonderful, when he once struck his theme, to see the lights play about him as from the better world he was nursing in his faithful old heart. But I used to say: "Old man, it is not practical. The world we live in is not ready for it. We shall have to wait until we get nearer the millennium. The time is not yet." Well, he had a small fortune he had got together as a working man and an inventor, for he was both; and, do what I would, I could not save him from investing the last dollar of it in his plan, just to make the demonstration, if he could do no more. It broke down. There was no help for this. Then he died of a broken heart, and went up to take his place by Antipas, the faithful martyr, and cry, "How long, O Lord, how long?"

Or it may be a man with a heavy burden and a weak back, a failing heart or brain and a sore battle, health for half a man and work for two men, tired when he wakes with a hard day before him, but quiet through it all, and with no thought of giving in, only of dying at his post; and he dies of the battle and the burden, faithful unto death.

Or your martyr, again, may be a woman, delicate and pure as they are in heaven, aspiring always and *always* driven back, earnest as Charlotte Brontë, self-forgetful as Mary Ware, brave as Lucretia Mott, yet hopeless in her fortune as Pucelle, the pure, white maiden of France.

Or she may be a wife and mother, borne down with heavy burdens, but bare of all sympathy or succor from the man who has brought them on her, and should clasp his arms about her now far more tenderly and surely than when he first won her love, her husband

and the father of her children. For what in the name of all that is most sacred in our life is the man good for who will load a woman down with the cares of a home and a family, and then let her fight the battle alone, while he is grumbling, as we used to say in Yorkshire, "like a bear with a sore head," shutting his heart, but not man enough to shut his mouth, and watching her die daily before his eyes, a poor, sad, home-made martyr, and then marrying again before a twelvemonth, let us hope, to a vixen, who will pay him back in his own coin, and serve him right?

Antipas, my faithful martyr, is here in the world, then, to-day, doing his work and dying when his time comes, with the light in his eyes,— yes, or with a cloud in his eyes, as it may please God,— but faithful all the same unto death; bearing the cross, but sure of the crown, or, what seems greater and grander still to me, bearing the cross, but *not* sure of the crown, and with never a thought that he is a martyr at all, yet entirely true to the last, and with no assurance of the waiting paradise in his poor, tired heart, only faithful unto death and to duty.

For this is where we touch the deeper pathos of these unknown and unnoted martyrs that they are so very often of such small account in their own thought of themselves and of what they can do. The youth who would not bend before the great golden God, it may be, in this very town, but went into the fire, all the same, and *did* burn; the Noah whose name has not floated across the wreck of a nameless deluge, but who had a boat, and, when the waters were out, filled her so full that she sank with all aboard, while he himself went down into the seething floods with them, and with as calm a heart as he ever had who floated safely to the crest of Ararat; the man who lay all his life by the pool of healing, but was never helped in and never made whole, yet who was just as patient and hopeful on the last day as the first; the Paul who was not sure he had fought a good fight, but died fighting; and the John who was also on Patmos, some sort of lone Patmos somewhere in this world, for the faith that was in him, yet never saw the open heavens and the city of God.

Antipas,— I knew him half a century ago; and he had it in him, *my* Antipas, to sing Psalms as sweet as "The Lord is my Shepherd," and to slay giants as big as Goliath of Gath. But he died almost before he could begin, yet never for a moment lamenting his early doom; and I closed his eyes, and wept by his grave. Antipas,— he was a minister who went West into Illinois about 1831 as a missionary, and was true as Daniel; but he had no visions to keep him in heart that he could tell you of, so he grew old in his wandering, and the people did not care to hear him then, but still the burden lay on him to preach the Word in season and out of season. And then one night, as he wandered over the vast, lone prairies in the winter, the wolves came howling after him; and he was no more seen of men.

Antipas,— long ago he used to come into the Western settlements of Pennsylvania in cider time, and load himself with apple pips, and then start westward again, no man knew where or on what errand. But, when the tides of emigration swept over the Ohio westward towards the great green lands, they found sunny spots by brooks and springs where there were little orchards of seedling apples fighting the wilderness; and a quarter of a century ago you could still find mossy patriarchs of that old man's planting,— who was a crank to the white man and a medicine man to the Indians, God's angel of the covenant, clad in skins. He saw the trend and the drift of the coming age and manhood and the new homes, and gave his life for these; but no man knows where or when he died, or how he went to see what they had to say about it who keep the accounts when his work on the earth was done, the beautiful, holy work.

Antipas,— Antipas was a woman who had an infirmity fifty years, and spent all she had also, on the doctors, and then died of her disease, after raising two small children who were no more to her, save for her loving and yearning old heart, than they were to you or me. They were born in sin, and then the mother died; and then my Antipas, the dear saint, mothered them, that was all, and maintained them by working at a mangle. I mind how I rushed into her cellar one day when I went over to see my mother, for we had worked together in the factory some years before, so I always went to see her in her cellar; and there she was kneeling with those little children, saying her grace before meat, while her "meat" was some dry bread and something you would call tea if you should make believe very much indeed, and that was all. But, when she was through, she rose, and whispered: "I was only saying my grace with the bairns, my lad. They will have a hard time when I leave them; and I shall have to go soon, and I want to teach them to be thankful, poor things, and myself, too, for I have a deal to thank God for, thou knows."

Antipas,— he was a rough in an English regiment when they took him prisoner, the heathen, and told him he might live if he would kotow before their chief. But he said, "Nāāy,"— the long-drawn Saxon nāāy,— "I'se an Englishman. I wēēant do nowt like that, and shame my sōōart. I can die, but I cannot do that." And so he died.

> "Fair Kentish hop-fields round him seemed,
>   Like dreams, to come and go.
> Bright leagues of cherry blossom seemed
>   One living sheet of snow.
> The smoke above his father's door
>   In low, soft eddyings hung.
> And must he watch it rise no more,
>   Doomed by himself, so young?"

There was but one way out of the trouble. He must not shame them there in the small cottage thousands of miles away: he must be a man, this poor fellow, who never knew he was Antipas.

Now, some lives pay their way close and clean to the end. Mine does, I know. So that if the High Powers should say, "We have nothing else for you here or hereafter," I think I should answer: "I make no claim. I would love to see those I have lost once more who are in the blessed heavens; but, if it is not to be so, I am still debtor for the untold blessing of my many years." So must many of us feel who have had such an even and happy lot as mine has been. We are no martyrs, or, indeed, we may not be of the stuff of which martyrs are made; and so it may be the dear God, Father of us all, chooses his men as a wise smith chooses his steel, mindful of the instrument he wants to make and use. I do not try to guess the divine reason for giving me the sunny side of the way. I only know it is so, and that he who rules in heaven has so far made no martyr of me, or put it in my way to be one, or, it may be, in yours; but what hosts there are who have never had our health or strength, or any gift at all except this of Antipas in the old days,—a steady courage to be faithful unto slaying, martyrs for God! And these, again, I think of most tenderly look for no reward in the blessed world to come. As I said, they are only eager to be true to their trust down here. They may see others of whom they are ready to say, as we say of them, "There must be an eternal love which will find these out finally, and give them their reward." It is never of themselves they think; and yet that loving instinct which would insist on a blessed outlook for these others, which would make the odds even, is not this the instinct pointing towards a divine life, in which they will all be partakers of this great glory, which flashes for a single moment and in a single line out of heaven, as it were, and shows us Antipas among the shining ones, disappearing here, but appearing there, forgotten on this side, but immortal on that, here a handful of dust, there the very instance of that which can never die, departing with a moan, but springing into life again with a Psalm?

And what I love better still to believe is this: that the dear God, our Father, will not let such men and women wait for the life to come after all before they know, in some dim, sweet fashion, what a glory rests on their unknown and unnoted life. Many a happy moment Antipas must have had before he went to the arena or the block, because this is what they all tell us whose experience is one with these obscure martyrs of every age. The great hope of the seeker, who never finds his great treasure in science or the arts, the great hope through which he trembles in expectation like a bird burdened with a carol; the euthanasia which steals over the poor martyr to duty at shy moments, and lights the pale face with a shining which is not of the sun. The near touch of heaven I felt in the presence of that poor old woman kneeling beside her mangle and asking a blessing on the crust and the thin ghost of the tea,— this is what my Antipas has for his bounty as he goes marching or stumbling to his unrecorded death, the great deep sea bearing up the poor little craft which is driving through the storm to the eternal rest and peace.

The story can never be told of these gleams, but this is what they mean. They tell the discoverer, who still cannot quite discover, how surely the thing is there all the time, waiting to be revealed; and he knows it is all right, though he may never get at the rights of it the longest day he lives. They touch fainting men and women in their weakness and pain, as the angel touched the prophet, and give them the heaven-baken bread, on the strength of which they go, also, their forty days in the wilderness. They are the proof before letters of the coming of the Lord, while the waiting heavens seem but a waste and "a space thick sown with alienated stars."

I treasure a little wood-cut by Millais of a woman standing within the clutch of the incoming tide. She is bound there, and the waters are rising about her. There is no hope for her: she is doomed, and must die. But her face is turned upward by just a thought, as we should say, and her eyes shine with a great sweet light. It does not occur to you as you look at her that she feels the waters creeping up about her, because her heart is in heaven; and under the picture you read these lines:—

> "Murdered for owning Christ supreme
> Head of His Church, and no more crime;
> But, for not owning prelacy
> And not abjuring Presbytery,
> Within the sea, tied to a stake,
> She suffered for Christ Jesus' sake."

That picture tells me the story I want to learn and need to learn about Antipas, my faithful martyr. The flames do not gather upon them or the waters devour them, after all, because God sees to it by a divine masterhood; and death is lost in victory.

So my thought points towards a few simple lessons,

and this is the first: We are not to think these martyrdoms came to an end when the world we live in came to the conclusion that

> "If a man's belief be bad,
> It will not be improved by burning."

Men and women die martyrs now as they died in the old bad days. It is not in the old brutal way, but it is just as painful; and martyrdom goes on in obscure corners still,— where a great truth or a great reform which will win the world to a better life in the long day of God finds my Antipas; where great discoveries, that hold in their hearts a vast benediction to man, haunt those who cannot but work at them until they drop in their tracks; in homes the law cannot touch, also, and in cellars and garrets where forlorn men and women would any day welcome death as a grand and blessed boon, but keep up their hearts and face their duty cheerfully. Some of them are as sure of heaven as if they were there; and some are rough, homespun men, of no vision and of the earth, earthy, until the great moment comes, and then they jam the wheel and run the boat ashore to save the passengers, dropping, when that is done, a burnt ember; keep their hand on the lever and mind the train, but are crushed in the deed out of all semblance of a man; leap into the furnace of a burning home after a woman or a little child, and come out no more. All martyrs, and all martyrs for God in duty and in a simple manhood, gathering their whole power into one spring for this and landing in the everlasting life, while they leave us to our disputes about who shall be saved, and becoming themselves the supreme instance in such supreme self-sacrifice, heedless of what we may say about their doom, leaving all this to take care of itself, but then doing more to enlarge and sweeten our ideas of God's saving grace in such noble saving, perhaps, than all our preaching.

And this is the second: that those of us who have some chance at helping or may have, by reason of our better fortune and lot, shall do what we can for these obscure and unnamed martyrs. It may not be much we can do; but we can do something, if it is only to say to them: "This is my fight, too; and I am with you in your forlorn hope, in your sad lot, in your pioneering. You have my sympathy. I am your friend." There can never be more than a handful in such a case, never more than the twelve; but, then, what a grand thing it is to count for one in the twelve, even if it be but the doubting Thomas, the least of them all! We can help those, it may be, who would fain hide some noble thought in the world's life, but cannot find the way to do it, or those who bear heavy burdens on weak backs, or those who, within the husk of a rough and, it may be, an evil life, still hold this kernel of nobility, while we may sing our Psalms and say our prayers, be proud of our churches and think our ministers are the very flower of the flock; but, if we do not keep our hearts open and warm towards these obscure martyrs, we are not of His heart by whose name we are called.

Do I speak to those, finally, who, as life opens and

duty begins to grow clear, will find it is hard and trying work to stand and fight for the outcast truth, for the unpopular reform, for anything that comes within the scope of my thought? Take heart, and go right on when that time comes. You may be troubled, do not be distressed; perplexed, you must not despair; persecuted, do not even imagine you are forsaken; cast down, you cannot be destroyed.

In the old monastic gardens which have lain to the wilderness these three hundred years, when they dig down deep and turn up the soil, flowers spring and bloom again which have been buried ever since the harrying of the monks; and so shall your sowing be. You will think no man cares,— well, then, God cares. That you can do no one thing worth a moment's memory; so, it may be, thought Antipas, my faithful martyr; so thought my poor old friend, kneeling in her cellar; but I told that story many years after to a great congregation in a church in her own town, and a little host of them flocked about me after the service, and said, "Yes, we mind old Nelly, too, and her wonderful gentle heart." And I found, as we talked of her, that she was preaching better sermons after she was dead all those years than most of us preach who are living.

And you may think this may end it all. You were never more mistaken. The great, full tides will bear up your bark, never fear; or the tempter may tell you how you will have twice as good a time if you will only give up half your manhood. *The tempter lies.* "It's dogged as does it," the poor day-laborer says to the parson in the story, when he finds him quite broken down; and, it may be, this will be all you can do, and all Antipas could do that day. Well, then, I will pray: "O God, make me as noble in my doing as some dogs I know of are in theirs; and I will win the day by sheer doggedness, but I will win the day."

THE GREAT DIVINE SERMON.

"He opened his mouth, and taught them. And, when he had ended these sayings, the people were astonished at his doctrine."—MATT. v. 2. vii. 28.

WHEN we find our way to the heart of the Sermon on the Mount, we love to believe that a divine inspiration has given to it the place it holds as the keynote of the Gospels.

It is so full of good cheer that, when we take it to our own hearts, we find our life is shorn of very many of the troubles we go half-way to meet, and so full of the divine truth and grace that it comes home to the sincere soul in some such way as a sum well done comes home to a man with a good head for figures; while, if we believed and accepted the truth it tells us, there would be no more trouble or dismay, either about the way of life or its consummation, and no painful surmise about the doctrines and dogmas which lie outside its sunny boundaries, because the inward life and light we may find there would make the whole earth luminous to the hearer as it was to the preacher, and as much of heaven as we need to see through the veil.

Fending and proving would seem to be poor work when we held conference with ourselves about its holy verities, as when the master put Euclid before Newton, and he said, "Yes, this is true, of course," and then went on to explore the deeper mysteries of which that was to him the alphabet, until he had weighed the mountains in scales also, and the hills in a balance, and taken up the isles as a very little thing.

It would be as natural for us to take the truth it holds into our hearts as it is for a healthy man to breathe the fresh air or eat good bread or drink pure water; while we should seek this or that holy word we may find here for the soul's sickness, as the creatures that live close to nature seek herbs for their hurts.

So I do not make light of the Scriptures when I say that, if the whole divine wealth of them besides could be lost, we should still have a Bible in this sermon, and should only be the poorer as those are poor who have no silver, let us say, but have still enough of gold to answer all their needs, or as those are poor who have no food to answer all their desires, but have still full and plenty of the bread and milk and of meat and fruit on which men grow strong for the work they have to do.

Thomas Hughes says preachers should calculate their sermons, as the astronomer makes his almanacs, to the meridian of the people and the place they are intended for; but the Sermon on the Mount, to my own mind, is true to all the meridians, because its noon and night find their parallel always on the lines where the Lord God is the sun. And so it is as true to my soul's windows as to any, and as true to any as to mine, running through all the latitudes and longitudes Paul thinks of when he says God, who made the world and all things therein, is not far from every one of us, seeing that in him we live and move and have our being.

And reasons are the pillars of your sermon, Thomas Fuller says, while similitudes are the windows that let in the light; and we all know this who have had much to do with preaching or hearing. Well, the reasons in this sermon stand deep and true to me as the pillars of heaven, while the similitudes that adorn it are as the windows of sapphire and crystal that glass the way to the suns and stars.

You must not tire your hearers with long sermons, Luther said; while, when George Fox heard one early in his life which lasted four hours, it was borne in on him by the spirit that preaching should be abolished. And yet it is hard for us to draw the line here, when one sermon of a hundred and twenty minutes shall seem shorter to your hearers than another of half an hour.

I still remember how a man with a grand craggy head and wonderful gray eyes would come down from the hills and preach to us in my youth, who would seldom let us off under the hour or the hour and a half; but I also remember how his sermons would often end for me in a great hunger to hear more and more, while with some of the brethren, who were apt to be brief, it was just the other way, for the time comes when you cannot catch even young birds with chaff.

But the Sermon on the Mount never torments

me, and never tires, because it is like the city the seer saw in his vision, of which he says the length and the breadth and the height of it are equal; while a great and venerable man told me once that, when you heard Dr. Channing read from it, you seemed to hear the sum of all true preaching. Its closing words, as he read them, touched you as if you were in the tornado. You saw the house built on the sand shudder down to its doom. It was the echo in our century of the wonder which astonished those who heard the matchless discourse which had come to the preacher instantly from God.

We are all aware also that a great many sermons, and some of ours no doubt among them, are like a glass of Missouri water. You must let them settle in some quiet place before you can see through them, and then there is a gritty and earthy substance you are bound to reject. But the Sermon on the Mount runs as clear as the springs that percolate and pour through the granite among the hills of New Hampshire.

Or you seldom hear a sermon in which you are not aware of a crevice in the preacher's mail through which you could lance him easily if you were at all so ruthless in your fence as he is in the charge, and especially when you are at odds about the doctrine. Or you can see by one swift glance that the whole structure of the sermon is poor and mean, and stands against the background of the truth he is there to tell, as the hut of the Arab stands against the grand outlines of Baalbec or Palmyra; but here is no earthy and gritty substance you are bound to reject, no crevice in the shining armor of proof, and no mean conclusion in the sermon which his voice

> "Hath here delivered words of heartfelt truth,
> Tending to patience when affliction strikes,
> To hope and love and confident repose
> In God, and reverence for the life of man."

But is it not true again that we all shrink in some moods from reading the searching sentences, because they are God's very truth, and because they smite us in a fashion against which we have no defence? We would fain tamper with them, or, if it were possible, blow them down the wind, or say they are true up to a certain point, and then file a bill of exceptions; or else we would creep into the shell of human inability, and wait for easier terms, as if we should ask the Most High to ordain new standards to meet our short weights and measures, or let the sun stand still for our backward planting and the rain hold up for our easy-going harvesting.

We balk at the Beatitudes, when this heart is in us. They challenge us too greatly, and mean too much until we mean more. "Blessed are the poor in spirit." Such poverty does not please us. We want all the treasures of the kingdom, if we could have them down on the nail. "Blessed are they that mourn." We do not think so. Mourning is not to our mind. We would wear our rue with a difference of exemption. "Blessed are the meek." We believe in striking back. No man shall push us to the wall. Your meek man is apt to be a milk-sop. And so it is with the whole blessed word. We have our own ideas about these things, and may say the sermon is divinely true, and then break down at the exordium.

We come to the divine Preacher in our need, and ask him to help us solve the painful problems of this human life, and help us on our way. Why have we to drink so deep betimes of these wells of Marah? How is it that we are subjected to this strain, in which one force drags us down, while the other draws us upward? and why are we so full of unrest about those things that are half within and half without, or are only seen as through a glass darkly? and ask whether the mark of rank in nature is the capacity for pain? What is the holy truth of God? Where is the perfect trust, and how shall we find the rest that remains? We come to him with these problems, and here in his sermon he offers us the master key; but we do not want to enter in through the door, after all. The demand on us is too severe; and we fall back on the thought that the true thing to do is not to fight, but to find a substitute, or wrench the holy word to our own purpose, and then bury the text in the commentary.

We cannot meet the monition, "Let thy garments be always white," and so we welcome the teaching that we can exchange our filthy rags, as we call them, in an instant for the white robes of the saints; or this, "Be ye perfect even as your Father in heaven is perfect," and so we seek this perfection not in ourselves, but in another.

Nor must we wonder at this once more when the truth that comes home to us in the divine sermon takes the meaning of an instant demand to be met at once by this perfection on our part, or we shall stand as convicts in the courts of the Most High. This is where the temptation comes in on the one side to find an imputed righteousness and on the other to be content with some lower standard of life and character, because we may think this is too high even to strive after.

And so it is as if your painter, standing face to face with one of the noblest pictures in the world, should say: "This will never do for me. I must choose one in which the lines are not quite so true or the form and color so perfect"; or as if a man, setting out to make a chronometer which shall be a glory to him and a praise, should reject one of those for his ideal you can carry round the world through frost and fire, to find it has not lost a moment, and take one for his pattern you have to guess at.

Now, to my own heart and mind, the Sermon on the Mount is the holy and perfect truth touching my life I am to strive after always and with all my heart. It is to be the inspiration and the standard for my striving, but never the despair when its words seem to challenge me to meet their august demand at once and forever, or I shall go to the wall. I know that this is of no more use than if I was learning to become an architect, and Angelo should rise from the dead, and say to me, "Now go to work at once, and build a cathedral equal to mine yonder in Rome, or quit this business."

Tell me I must attain to this perfection in life and life's worth the first time I try, and then I cannot even try, poor creature as I am, any more than I would try to lift the great Krupp gun; but tell me this is the standard to which I may attain, that I find in my sermon the challenge, the inspiration, and the incentive, the mark and prize of my high calling I shall hold in my heart, and never dare to say this is good enough so long as I fall short of its light and leading, and that this is not to be done by my own lone self, but that all heaven is on my side, and is bound to see me win soon or late. Then I shall begin to find the true meaning and purpose of the Sermon on the Mount.

The divine worth of it for me will lie then in my steadfast purpose to be so perfect, and in the way I set my face and step out; for let this be settled once for all, and then there may be better men than I am in this attainment, yet they shall not be so good, because I may be pushing forward while they are falling back.

This is the trouble I find in the later pictures of one great master, because even with my poor insight I can see how he has lost track in them of the old striving after the perfection which makes his earlier work so wonderful to me, and so welcome, I see how there was a time when it was his meat and drink to do the will of God, and is painting his matchless pictures moved by the holy spirit of sincerity and truth; but, then, you can see how the time came when he would gain the whole world, and lose his own soul. But another whose work is a perpetual delight to me was striving onward, while he was falling backward; and so, while for some space there was no comparison between the old master and the new, there was this deep distinction,— that the one was pressing onward toward the mark and the prize of his high calling, while the other was backsliding, and did not care.

Now, this is the divine secret to me of the sermon as the standard and incentive for your life and mine. We may know very well that we have not attained or are already perfect to the line of its demand; but the question is, Do we want to be and mean to be, and are we trying now to touch even the hem of this pure white robe?

When one said to the old master, "I cannot see in nature the glory you have hidden in that picture," he answered, "Do you not wish you could, then?" Now this may be my trouble as I hear the Master say, "See those lilies, watch those birds, and see how your Father which is in heaven cares for them"? When I look up, and cannot see what he saw, is there any hunger in my heart to be one with him in the vision? or is there a chasm between us I do not care and do not try to pass, as he sits there still and speaks to me, and would have me be one with him, as he was one with the Father? The Sermon on the Mount is not the despair, I repeat, but the inspiration, for your life and mine. Had it not been possible for us to reach upward toward its holy bidding and meet its holy claims, it would never have been preached. The preacher never wastes his words as we do. Very often they may mean more than he could pack into that poor folk speech he had to use, but they never mean less. He is sincere with us as the day.

And so there is something very sweet and true to me in the loyalty of good and sincere men, who are troubled in watching the drift of the times, to the great divine sermon. They want what we all want, stand where we will and believe as we will,—a sure word from Heaven, a "Thus saith the Lord," now that the Scriptures have been called into court and questioned as to their absolute or their essential truth.

There is no sure refuge any more in the claim of their verbal infallibility. The proof is in and accepted that they are not wholly divine, but that many things in them are only human, and some fall short of that; while we must find what is divine in the whole sum of them, as we find the gold in the earth and dross.

Human souls are floating out on the waste waters of negation, and the age is asking, "What is truth?" with a new accent; and the answer comes from men with this heart in them, and insight, "Here is *truth* beyond all question, with the dew of heaven on it and the untouched bloom," and they say, "We will hold on right here until we have taken our bearings to the divine sermon and the truth it reveals," and so it becomes in some sort their catechism and creed.

This was the stand made by the fathers of our own faith, and the standard about which they gathered. They must find the truth from God which would command their deepest reverence and purest loyalty. They found it in this sermon and in other Scriptures as true to its lofty harmony as the notes in your perfect octave; and then they said, "Exhaust such truths as these or get beyond them in your quest for the truth of God." You can exhaust the ocean sooner or get beyond the stars. Despise them, look down on them! You can despise geometry sooner, when you want to catch the secret of the constellations or neglect them. You can neglect sooner the sowing of fine wheat and the baking of good bread.

So we may think we have gone far beyond the fathers of our faith now that light has come into the world touching a great many questions they did not dream of fifty years ago. And this may be true; but is not this true also,— that we have none of us risen so high that we can look down on these blessed teachings for our faith and life? Some things are always and eternally true,— just as true before they are revealed as they ever can be afterwards; and the truth I find here holds this worth to me in its heart, and when I fall back on it, if I will answer to its inspiration and life that may be, as when in the contest a young athlete falls back that he may strive forward to a finer purpose.

But the years have taught me for one that we can make no graver mistake than this we may make when we cleave to the letter rather than the spirit, so that the sermon shall become not a living word to us and whole, but a collection of dogmas and instances, in which we miss the whole beating life which lies within its heart. It must be to us all as it is with my true artist, if I may bring him up again, who will not dwell with the grandest picture in all the world to his mind that he may learn to copy merely, because there is a noble ambition in his soul to create. He wants to find the spirit and life there in its wholeness; and, while he may never hope to surpass the master, if there is a true heart in him and ambition, the time is sure to come when he will be a mere copyist no longer, but one who will do his own work in his own way, calling no man master.

And so it must be with our reverence and loyalty even to the great divine sermon. It must be fluent and plastic to each man and woman, and have no power or purpose of crowding us down or of cutting and clipping away at us, as if we were so many plants in an old Dutch garden, because there is no true growth in grace for us then. It is a grand, free outline, inviting and inspiring my own growth toward the perfection of the Father on the lines of my own nature; and, to be worthy its demand, I must stand true to this free spirit and imperial word, and I must bring to it or find in it an imperial soul.

It is no machine like those that turn out the watches. It is as the seed and tilth, the sunshine and shadow, the insight and oversight, and the seasons which bring forth the harvest home. So let me be sure of this; and then, when I want to find some sure word of God to help and inspire me, when my life is full of trouble and dismay, and heart and flesh fail, I will sun my soul in the Beatitudes, or if I would touch the very nerve of cleanness or of gentleness or of the love which never faileth. If I want to give so that it shall be like God's own giving, or would pray so that the answer shall abide within the asking, or to trust in the eternal love which clasps my life all about and the eternal providence which holds me fast, let me take the sermon to my heart; and it shall be with me as when Luther saw the small birds swinging on the spray in the gloaming, and flying forth in the morning, singing their song, and quite sure of their provision for the day, because they were sure of themselves.

Or, when I would find what worth abides in this system of faith or that, in this Church or another, High Church or Low, narrow or broad, this claim founded on the divine authority or that on the divine reason, the true inward light, here I shall be sure to find the true answer to my question in the sermon which has outlasted the pride and glory they were carving in marble and moulding in bronze when the words came floating on the breath of a summer's day from his heart who spake as never man spake.

The Sermon on the Mount has come unscathed through the fires of time, clothing itself in purer meanings and winning nobler intepretations. Our little systems have grown and ripened, and left their seed to be sown again for finer harvests; but this abides as it was gathered from those who had treasured it in good and honest hearts, sincere and sweet, forevermore, as the bread which cometh down from heaven.

Men also and churches have deformed it by false interpretations, twisted it into uncouth meanings, and degraded it, as when you cast pearls before swine; but the jewels have taken no taint, because the sermon holds within itself the light of heaven as the great rose diamond does, and with the light the freshness and sweetness as of the spring. And so I love this loyalty of the deeper heart in our time to the sermon, and would share it. I find in it a constitution within which I can be God's free man, and a creed, if I need one, so large and inclusive that I need feel no fear about being left out of the number of those who want to witness a good confession touching their faith in God and his Christ. It affords for me a rule of life which must be true and good in any world to come and of faith which will stand all weathers in

> "This age that blots out life with question-marks,
> This nineteenth century with its knife and glass,
> That makes truth physical, and thrusts far off
> The heavens so neighborly to man of old
> To space sparse sown with alienated stars."

WHY SIMON PETER WENT A-FISHING.

"Simon Peter said to them, I go a-fishing."—JOHN xxi. 3.

SIMON PETER was a fisherman when the Master found him, and called him to be an apostle; while not long ago he was dreaming of a day near at hand when the Messiah would drop his disguise once for all, reveal his divine mission and authority, drive the powers then in possession of his holy land to the wall, and establish a kingdom in which he who had been a mere fisherman on the lakes would be a prince in Israel and hold the wealth of the world at his command.

How his family fared in those times we do not know, but may still imagine it would be rather hard now and then to make ends meet, as it is so often still, if the bread-winner is a dreamer when he should be a worker, and by all means hold the home well together, though it be at the cost of the kingdom which is seething in his heart and brain like new wine in the vat. But the dream has come now to a rude and woful waking. The kingdom is not of this world. So much is clear at last. This is all he can be sure about. The rest is hidden in a mist.

There was some money also before the fearful sorrow struck them which ended on the cross; but this vanished with Judas, who had the bag. So it is clear again that something must be done, and done quickly, for bare bread, or they will starve; and, as all the ways are closed except the one which leads down toward the beach and the boat, he was fain to say, "I go a-fishing."

And I think he must have made up his mind to return to the old craft and calling also through the conviction, which would grow strong in him, that this was all he was good for now.

There was a time not long ago when the Master had said, "Thou art Cephas, and on this rock I will build my church, and the gates of hell shall not prevail against it." But he had made fearful work of his faith and life since that day in denying the best and dearest friend he had in all the world, when he should have stood to his colors like a brave and true man, and defied the mob to do its worst.

Indeed, it was only the other day that he had said he would die with him and for his sake, but had broken the promise shamefully. Yet, as there was still the making of a very grand man in him, as we know, he was smarting for it now, and calling himself by all sorts of evil names. But now in the very crisis of his shame and self-abasement there came to him one little gleam of light, if I have caught the true thread of his story. He must have said to himself: "There is still one thing you can do to hold your own like a man among men. You can go back to your old craft and calling on the water. The thrones and dominions may have all been a delusion and a snare, but there is no delusion in the old boat and the nets.

You thought you were a man who could win in every battle. You were a mere poltroon in a fight like that you had to face the other day; and now, if God wants men to do his work in this world, you can be sure he will not want you. The Master said, 'Thou art rock,' while you see you are a mere heap of shifting sand; but you do know all about storms and how to handle a boat in the worst that ever came sweeping down from the hills, while, if you are beaten in the last and worst, please God, you will know now how to die a man's death, though you have failed to live a man's life. So you can take to your old calling again, to win, it may be, some new grain of the self-respect in it you have lost, and prove yourself a man after all." And so he said, "I go a-fishing."

Nor can I doubt that this was the very best and wisest thing he could do that day,— to fall back into the old grooves of the home again and the good day's work, because rest would be found in the work, help in the home, and the healing he could hope to find nowhere else in the world just then.

We may well believe his wife could have no great sympathy with his dreams of thrones and kingdoms, while, it may be, it was so hard for her to keep the home together and find milk and bread for the children; still, when he came home after that woful night in the judgment hall, with the pain and shame of it in his heart and eyes, the good wife and mother then would rise to the great and royal demand.

The whole world might cry shame on him now, but not this one woman. She knows what she has to do in this sore crisis. She has to come close to his side, to stand by him like a true comrade, and help him the best she knows. Have we not all known such good women, standing in the forlorn hope shoulder to shoulder with such men, when to our thinking it was against all reason? and we say, "The man deserves his doom," while our hearts beat with a proud and tender sympathy for the woman, and we said, "Gabriel, the great angel, could fight no such battle."

So I wish I could paint you a picture of that going home, and recall the sweet, low tones that would run through her words of welcome and the gentle light that shone in her eyes, the steadfast loyalty revealed in many ways with that eager welcome, yet not over-eager, lest his pride take fire, with never a hint of "I told you so," or "This is what your dream of the thrones and kingdoms has come to" from those loyal and loving lips.

And so to take to the boat again and the fishing was to take to the home in this one true way, as men must do who know what is best for them, when hope burns low, when pride is broken, when joy is slain, and they imagine they have not one friend left on the earth or in heaven.

They have one friend left. We have all one friend left then, who are so blessed as I shall not doubt this man was,— the woman who will help us when we seem to have no strength and courage left to help ourselves. Yet I am not sure that he thought of this indeed, only of taking right hold, first of all, where he had left off, and taking home his load of fish for a token of what lay in his heart; and, when this was done, the rest would be done by indeed the better half.

It was a wise and good thing again for him to say, "I go a-fishing," as I think, when I try to find the man's heart through my own. Because this would not only solve the question of the daily bread, reveal what real manhood was still in him, and bring him home to his own fireside, where he would find gentle hands to heal his hurt and the presence of the wife and children to lure him out of the pain, but it would take him back to Nature, the good mother and helper of us all.

So he would go out on the water with his trouble; and the mother would rock him on the waves, would soothe him with cool winds, and shine down gently on him in the night from her stars, whispering such peace as could come to him then from her heart helping him to forget his trouble for a while perhaps, and so tone to-morrow half a note higher than to-day.

It was a wise and good thing for him to do also, when we think of the wonder which had stormed the very citadel of his life since Easter morning. Here was the risen spirit of the dear Friend and Master in this world again, stealing out from within the veil, burning through the shadows of death, touching them in the living presence, and winning them to the conviction they lived henceforth and died to maintain, that death had no dominion and the grave no victory over his living soul. That the man should be bewildered by the wonder when it touched him, and feel as if the use and wont of life was no longer to be trusted on the land, would be quite natural; and so he would take to the water, because your true sailor always draws a deep line between his own familiar element and ours, and expects to get his bearings on the water he may have lost on the land.

There could be no mistake about the fishing, and no mystery about the honest old craft. She would answer to the tiller and go before the wind; while the winds and waters and the night would be all about him and familiar to his shaken heart, and real. So he must have said: "Let me do this, and I shall know where I am and what I am about. Then, if the dear Friend and Master should come to me there, and find me hard at work, as I was when he called me in the old days to follow him, it will be the best proof I can give him now of what manhood remains in me after my shameful treason in the hall, when I went out weeping bitterly." And so he said, "I go a-fishing."

These, then, are among the reasons that come home to me, as I try to find the man's heart through my own, why he should take to the boat and the day's — or shall we say the night's? — work; and now, if this was the last word we were ever to hear about him, should we not all be ready to say: " Poor troubled brother, you made bad work of it that night in the hall, but there can be no mistake about this you mean to do now.

It is far better for you to be out in the boat, the bread-winner, as things stand with you now, than to be shut up in your chamber on your knees, because all the prayers you can say from this to sunrise will not bring a pound of meal or a bowl of milk for those you have to fend for there in the home.

Better by far be grasping the tiller, minding the sail, and hauling at the nets than folding your hands or beating them on your breast in despair. This labor is prayer in the pass to which you have come, this lake your kingdom, and this boat your throne. Better be fishing than reading your Bible, even if you own one, because what a man brings to his Bible is of quite as deep a moment very often as what he finds in it. You might take to those rose-colored glasses again for the reading, as so many do in your case, and go to hunting up all the passages in your prophets about the thrones and kingdoms, which would lead you to imagine you were right, after all, about the dream, and all you had to do was to wait where you have now made up your mind to work.

You can give no better proof that a new life is stirring in your heart which will make you a prince of a grander type than all your dreams, no better proof than this you give in taking hold again down at the base line of your life and fortune. You have got your lever all right now, and may yet do your noble stroke at lifting the world; for the one thing for a man to do, first of all, is to be true to the duty of the day, and that means for you the care of his home and family."

So runs my thought of some reasons why Simon Peter said, "I go a-fishing"; and now shall we try to see what he might have said and done, trying still to find the clew to his life through our own, and what we might be tempted to do in some such case?

The man had been nursing a faith in God, as he thought, which but a few days ago seemed to be as firm as the earth he stood on and as true as the arches of the heavens. It seems that he had pawned his home on it and all he had in the world in the assurance that he should be amply and gloriously rewarded, only to find he was utterly mistaken, when his dream had burst like a shining bubble, and the thrones and kingdoms were a mirage which had gone down with the sun.

His hopes had soared as on the wings of eagles, centring all in Simon Peter and his kith and kin. They were shot through the heart by these awful arrows of disaster, and lay dead about his feet. Yes; and his love was so deep just now that he had stood ready to die for the proof of it, so he said, but the one brief hour had proven it was self-love, very mean also and poor at that, and so the love had gone to wreck with the faith and hope.

Now we may have all known those, or may be of them, who, when this befell, would not feel after a surer faith, a diviner hope, and the love which never faileth, which is only another name for the love of

God, but would take a more dogged grip on what we call realities, and make these the great aim and end of life; and Simon could have done this when he said, "I go a-fishing."

He could have said, "I have come to grief and sore loss through my dream, and am as poor as poverty; but minted gold is good and lands and houses. So I will make money now, and have those, because they are real things; while I notice that nowadays men are usually esteemed and exalted not so much for their worthiness as for what they are said to be worth."

So he could have lived his life and done his work, worshipping the golden calf the while, — an easy thing for one of his race to do, you say; but I answer, "Not one mite easier for one of his race than for one of ours." Still, he could have done this; and then a day could have come when they would have called in the priest, the doctor, and the lawyer, — for this was the end of all his labor under the sun, — and the mourners would go about the streets, and the people say: "He made a blessed end. Lo, this money left to the synagogues and the temple, a clear tenth of all he was worth!" This he could have done for a nine days' wonder, but there would be no more trace of him to-day than there is of his dust.

But let us see now what the drift and trend was from sundown that day when he said, "I go a-fishing," to the day when he saw the sun set for the last time on this earth.

He went back to such realities as were left for

him when his life had suffered that sad wreck, and would try to make a living, because this was all he could do just then. He would anchor the boat to his doorstep, take her out, earn his bread, and try to find his bearings; but this was not all he would do. He carried with him an eager and wistful heart, which was opening toward a new and nobler life even then; and it was right there among the realities he could still trust that the deeper and diviner realities began to take his soul captive.

He went back to his day's work, and thereby found his way to his throne and princedom; back to nature, and found God and his risen Christ; back to the lowest place, and was bidden to the highest; back to the fisher's cottage, and there the way lay to the many mansions; back to the inland lake, and its outflow was that river the streams whereof make glad the city of God.

He found through his treason that Simon Peter was a very poor stick for the pilgrimage, when it was all and only Simon Peter, bent on being the greatest after the king in the new kingdom of God on the earth.

But the old pride in Peter had passed away, I take it; and he had no ambition then beyond a simple and manful life. And a weary way it was from that turning! but it lay straight and true for him from there to the eternal home,—a lonely way, yet it was peopled for him with the dear divine presence and the celestial companions; and a sad way often, but then the joy was so much more than the sorrow; and a way terrible to the flesh as walking through fire. Yet, they say, he begged for the boon of a deeper misery when he must die, which would set the seal for all time and to all men touching the perfect sincerity of his sorrow for the great treason in the hall so long ago, for which the dear divine Friend had long ago forgiven him, but for which he had never forgiven himself; and then all heaven came into his heart, and shone from his eyes.

Faith was perfected, hope soared far above the boundaries of earth and time, and love was one with faith and hope, and their glory and crown, and all harking back, if we will but think of it, to that time when the poor tried man said, "I go a-fishing."

Many years ago, in a great historic city, I went to see a picture painted by Rubens for the church where he was baptized. It was the altar-piece, and I must pay a fee to see it. I had been paying money right and left all day to see things until I was as cross as a bear and sick of the whole business. Still, I must see it on their terms, so they turned it to the light of the setting sun. And I remember how I stood there in the silence for a few moments to find I was sobbing and trying to force back my tears. It is the picture of Peter's death on the cross, as he had prayed he might die, and, as you look, the pain smites you as with a solid stroke; but this was not the reason for the tears. I saw only those eyes presently in which the master has hidden such deeps on deeps of victory, mastering the agony, that you stand there in amaze.

The wonderful clear gray eyes are looking from the tree right into the heart of heaven, and the light in them is more than the shining of the sun. It is the light which lights the sun, the light of God.

He knows nothing of the pain. Death has no dominion there. The curtains of time are falling. The eternal life fills the fainting and failing heart. He is absent already from the body and present with the Lord. You feel this is no mere fancy of the master, it is the living truth about the man, caught by the hand of genius to touch all hearts; and then you think of the lines touching the first martyr, how

> "Looking upward, full of grace,
> He prayed, and from a happy place
> God's glory smote him on the face."

And now there are many lessons to be drawn from this whole matter for which I have scant time; while to me the best of them is this I have tried to open, and which rests and turns on the good resolve of the man, "I go a-fishing,"— that my own true day's duty is the most blessed thing for me in all the world. Have I been dreaming to my loss and theirs who look to me, and done treason through my dreams to God and his Christ and to my own soul? Here are the first conditions of a truer manhood waiting in my sorrow and shame in my day's nearest duty.

Am I in trouble, feeling that all the stanchions and safeguards on earth and in heaven have given way? The first stroke I can make for a new and nobler reality lies for me also in the day's instant and imperative duty. Do the great mysteries touch me with their pain of life and death and the life to come?

I must not go running hither and yonder to have them solved. They will open to me while I stand by my duty week-day or Sunday and my day's work for God and man.

Is there some grander destiny waiting for me, as there was for this man? I can win out of my very sin and shame and by rugged ways, and hard as they were for him. The princedom, the throne, and the crown, rest still and forever on the simple and true day's duty and the good day's work, though it be no more there and then than this Simon Peter held in his heart when he said, "I go a-fishing"; for still

> "The path of duty is the way to glory."

JOHN THE BELOVED.

"Lord, what shall this man do?"— JOHN xxi. 21.

IT was for John the beloved that Peter felt this loving concern; while we may well believe the reason for this distinction "the beloved" would begin to draw them together very early in their life, as they were first cousins on the mother's side, Mary and Salome being sisters, if we are right in our surmises.

Their love has come to its perfection in the time since Jesus found John and his brother busy with their boat, and asked them to join him. They went with him, as it seems, asking no questions; while from this time we can trace the truth that they were nearer to each other, and dearer, than all the world beside.

John was with him in the transfiguration on the mount, leaned on his breast at the last supper, and was one of the three nearest to him in the garden; while he was the one man among them all who had fronted the danger when the first blind terror was spent and he came to himself. He had stood close to the cross then, with the hapless women, and had taken his dear friend's last will and testament to his heart, that he should look after the poor mother who stood beside him, heart-broken, and then, when all was over, had taken her home to his own house, to love her and care for her to the end of her life.

So we may see how the matter stands, and how natural it would be the good comrade should ask his question, What shall this man do? The life they have lived together through these years has been so blended into one life by their love that Peter finds it hard to imagine even how the one can be in heaven and the other abide so forlorn on the earth.

How shall he be able now to stand alone, much less go on alone, through the years that remain? and so what shall he do? The time was when he would have been able to bear the burden as well as the rest of them, or, it may be, better; for he was so strong and vital they had called him the Son of Thunder, while it was no small thing three years ago to give up his living, as Peter had done also, at the Master's bidding. But this is giving up his life, as it lay in this which was taken while he was left; and so what shall he do?

John Paul says, when one he loved better than a brother was dead, "I did not ask why I had lost him, but how it was that I should ever have found him"; and then he could only be grateful and glad through his pain. But no such thought as yet touches the good comrade. He has not begun as yet to realize what he might still be to them all who had passed through the gates of death into the immortal life. He only sees the poor friend standing there, as I think of him, a broken man, not yet in his full prime; and, if he should live through many years yet, what shall he do? He has lost the personal human presence nearest him in all the world,—lost the nobler and better half of himself, shall we say, lost what makes his life worth living, and now the light of the days will never be again what it has been, or the joy. He may live, and must; but in all he does henceforth they will miss the splendid stroke of the Son of Thunder. His strength will fail at the spring of its inspiration; and so what shall he do?

So I think we should read the truth, as it lies between the lines of the question and the answer, who may have struck some such sorrow and loss — and then we may see how the truth is as old as life — and the severing of these close and warm and most loving human ties.

And as the question, What shall this man do? was not singular and separate from our life, no more, as I think of it, is the answer. This may be as full of all heartening to us now, and as true as it was to John the beloved, when we fall on this sorrow, though as yet we may be no more able to understand or take it home to our hearts than he was that day. If I will that he tarry till I come,— this is the answer; and then the curtain falls on the troubled man who will have to face his life, as the good comrade thinks of him, shorn of the strength and joy which gave life its choicest worth.

The curtain falls, but it is lifted again, and often, in John's long lifetime; and then we can see by glimpses and glances what this tarrying means to him, and what it may mean to you and me.

He must wait for his own sake, first of all, as the grapes that ripen late must stay on the vines, and the fruits long a-mellowing must stay on the tree. For, when we follow him in the Gospels down to this day, we may see quite easily he is by no means the man we think of as John the beloved, because he was the gentlest and most loving among them all, the man who wins his way to their hearts and ours because he holds this beautiful gift in present possession through a nature which is as the vine clinging and climbing sunward by tender tendrils of love which must so hold and cling. The dear divine Friend who loves him so calls him a Son of Thunder; and such a name can hardly have been given to the man we have always in our mind.

The truth is he was a bigot at times of the old, stern type, as we may see when we read our Gospels. He would have the Master call down fire from heaven once, to burn up a town where the folk did not give them good welcome, because they were of another church and denomination, and had to take the rebuke with the rest of them, "Ye know not of what spirit I am: I have not come to destroy, but to save." And again, when he finds one healing the sick who is not one of the little band, he will have him hindered; but again the Master rebukes him by the word: "He that is not against us is for us. Let the man alone."

This is the John who must tarry, as he stands in the Gospels, with his whole love, such as it was, centred in the dear Friend and Master alone; and, when we trace him in the early traditions through many years of his tarrying, he is still about the same man.

He goes to Ephesus, and falls out sadly, with the little church which has been gathered there, on some points of doctrine, and falls into something very near of kin to a rage. We hear rumors again about his helping a mob to destroy one of the heathen temples, and of his doing some other things which help us to see how long the fruit must tarry on the tree of his life before it will be ready for the gathering, large, ripe, and mellow and sweet to the core, the true grafting on the true vine.

But, then, we follow him again, to find quite another man, when the time and tarrying have done their perfect work, gentle and loving to our full desire, and sweet of heart to the core.

One of these traditions I love best to read and take to my heart. The brigands were out, and were harrying the farms and homesteads under the leadership of a man who had been very dear to him many years before, and one of his flock. John the beloved is very old and feeble then, they say; but he insists on going alone to find this man, and win him back to God and holy ways, if loving can do it, and all gentleness. So he finds him at last; but he is no more the Son of Thunder: he has found the first secret of his tarrying, though he shall never find another, that,

> " Except we are growing gentle and good,
> There can be no good in our growing old."

He talks to the brigand, who flees from him at first while still he follows, just as the dear Friend would have talked to him in the old time. He will not smite the iceberg with the thunderbolt of a divine wrath, but will melt it, please God, with the love of Christ, which is one now with his own; and so the man breaks down, kneels at the old saint's feet, begging to be restored, and then returns with him to his home and to a new life.

Then we watch him through the glass of the traditions, a wonder of old age, sitting in the sunshine, with a bird on his shoulder which flutters down to feed out of his hand; and the people about him wonder how so great a man should love so small a creature. And, when the long tarrying is almost over and done with, we hear how he will have them carry him to the church once more, because he cannot walk now, he is so old and feeble. So they take him there, and set him, like a child, in the midst; while all he can say to them is, "Little children, love one another," with a sweet and beautiful repetition which is perfectly fitting and true to him, when you think of the man he was. "Little children, love one another." This holds all the law and the gospel for him now in the ripeness of the hundred years; and then we see him no more. He closes his dim eyes on this world of ours forever, and goes his way to find the dear divine Friend again, who left him so long ago.

So this was what came of the tarrying. The Son of Thunder turned into sunbeams of loving kindness and tender mercy; and this was the answer made good to the comrade who had thought of him as the one man among them all for whom life could hold no more of worth, when he said so pathetically, "What shall this man do?"

He shall do this, is the answer: he shall grow gentle in all gentleness and lovely in all loving, so that the old, harsh fires and thunders will be quite forgotten or not minded through all time to come, and then leave the treasure he has won in a Gospel which shall enrich our life forevermore; for, while we may not be able to prove to all comers he wrote the Gospel as we have it now, we cannot doubt that his heart beats through it, and the wealth of his loving memories.

So I have been moved to touch the question, and answer this Easter morning, because the truth they hold comes home to so many of us who fall on this sore trouble of a severed and broken life, in which we seem to have nothing to live for now; while those who think of us, and pity us, may be saying, "What shall this man do, or this woman, left like a bird in the net, while its mate is soaring and singing in the heavens so far away?" If the dog cannot live away from his master, he can lie down on the grave and die; and the bird, if he takes his loss to heart over-much, you find him dead some morning in his cage. They begin again, and their life is presently made good to them as ever; or, if they cannot do that, they die. But there is no such way out of the trouble for us, save as Heaven makes one; and so what shall we do, this is the question, while the answer may come to us in many ways, but they all centre, first of all, right here about the old blessed word, What if *they* tarry till I come?

For does it seem to be indeed a broken life I am watching, or possess shorn of the choicest treasure? Then the many years have been teaching me this truth: how the time may come to us, if we can wait for it patiently, when we do not take hold of life again in the old strong fashion, but life takes hold of us in some diviner fashion, as it took hold of this John the beloved.

It is as when you come to the bar and have to wait for the tide, which waits for the power from on high, that lends the lift of another world, and, lo! you are in deep water. It is as when we sail away toward the old home of the race, and you see some day a faint line far away you know is not a cloud; and then, as the night comes on, a light shines, and that means the fulfilling of the promise. It is like the grain sown in the fall of the year, which sprang into life and the fair promise of the harvest home; but the sun retreated, the mists came down, the frosts followed, and the great snows lay white on the land. The storm swept over all, the growth was stayed, and the hope that is seen lay under the hard and bitter winter.

But the wheat has been waiting in those poor blue blades, hidden down under the drifts, while the roots have been growing stronger for the tarrying. And now here is the sun returning. While the drifts have melted, the blades are taking on their tender green again, and shooting forth afresh toward the heavens; and on a day we can well foresee the choice word will be said down there in the market, " This is winter wheat, and the best we handle." The most noble secret of its worth lies in the tarrying until the sun returns to draw it forth, and the warm rains fall on it: then the ears unfold their golden banners in the summer tide, and all is well. Yes, and all is well through waiting.

So, "What shall this man do, or this woman?" we may say, with the pathetic concern of the old saint in the making. Their life is arrested, their joy is slain, their hope has gone out or burns very low and dim, their sun has retreated in the heaven of their life, the clouds are down on them, and the mists, the frosts, are on them, and the snows of winter. What shall they do?

Well, it is written for us all what we shall do. What if we shall tarry till he come again, the sun of our hope and joy?

Nature has her blessed parable ready for our reading of the holy worth of waiting. So is it true that all things come to those who can wait: then here, of all the times that can come to us, it is true, here may be the finest wealth won by waiting. "I will have none of this," the arrested blade may say. "Let me die, and have done with it. I am buried under the drift. What is there for me but the end of all hope and joy?" "But no," the brave germ answers in the heart of all,— not here alone in the highest life and divinest, but on all the lines,— "I am not here to die, but to wait, and then to live to some finer purpose."

This is where the painter finds his finest pictures, the inventor his insight, the preacher his choicest word, the true king his power to rule with Alfred in the name of the Lord, the President his strength to lead the people: these all answer to the parable of the brave, enduring grain.

"No, no," the brave heart, and hopeful, answers, "I must bear all this, and wait. There is something for me beyond these clouds and mists that lie so heavy, these storms and drifts which strike like the stroke of doom, yes, and the retreating sun,— something beyond and above them all. Ay, and something in them of God's treasure, and so I will wait." And then the time of fruition comes, and we find as the good old man did the worth of the tiny word *if* he tarry. For the kingdom of heaven is as when a man casteth seed into the ground, and it springeth and groweth, he knoweth not how, first the blade, then the ear, and after that the full corn in the ear.

Let me take this Easter lesson to my heart, then, as it rests first in the question, What shall this man do? What he did was to tarry, and nourish his heart on the faith that the dear and divine Friend would be with him always, even unto the end of the world, and then go forth in the faith to live his life, to do his work, and to learn his lesson, how to become sweet of heart, and gentle, who had been so often harsh and masterful, how to melt where he would once have burned with fire, and how to persuade where aforetime he would have hurled the thunderbolt to slay.

It all came to him, stealing in like the light and warmth of the early sun, the life which was hid with Christ in God, and won him at last, and held him to all gentleness and love. He could have said: "What is the use waiting? I am no good, bare of his presence and the clasp of his hand. His breast to lean on, and the loving glance from his eyes as we went on our way, nay, his very voice in rebuke was more to me than any other voice ever was in praise. And so what shall I do or what can I do but go lamed and out of heart through the years that remain, and then die?"

But he held up his head and his heart to face life again, and waited; and then he found life was waiting for him, and the work to which he had been called and elected.

He had been a follower. He had done with this, and must be a leader in the holy way of life and of God. An inquisitor he must be, a man with a heart in him, great, generous, and hospitable toward all goodness and truth; for this lay in the sealed orders, "*If* he tarry till I come." He had been a bitter partisan in spots: he must grow catholic as God's sunshine. He was always strong: he must learn now to be gentle. He must be to the waiting world in his stead who came to show us the Father, and then all the beatitudes fell like the gentle rains upon his good white head.

And, then, if I may touch one more tradition, a day came when they gathered from far and wide to where his home was, and said to him: " You are the last man on the earth who saw the Master, and were nearest to him of all the disciples. But these reports we have of him as he lived and spoke do not seem to tell the great divine story in all its fulness. They are very good, as far as they go; but something is left out. We have heard you tell how he washed your feet once, just before he was taken away; and there were many wonderful and comfortable words he said in those last days we have heard you repeat these many years, for you seem to forget nothing which belongs to the far-away time. Now may we not write it all down from your own lips before you leave us to find him who has risen and is with God?" Well it was so they tell us who handed down the traditions, and so we have this Gospel of the loving heart which finds its spring-head in the heart of John the beloved.

And now, to us all who will, this may be the tenor, the treasure, and the blessedness of our waiting when the human tie is broken,— that, through our patience and faith, it may become divine.

We can live so nobly, not in despite of the great sorrows and bereavements, but because of them, that our life shall be a gospel, though we can never write or frame one with our lips.

Some do not grow larger of heart and life, and sweeter, but sterner and more bitter; and then, alas! for the tarrying. But others grow, as this man did, gentle and fair and full of all charity, pouring out their pent-up love on the many they had given to one who is no more; and then that is their answer to the question, What shall this man do, or that woman? They are in their way as he was in our sister city, who, when his one daughter died in her early beautiful womanhood, poured out his wealth and what remained of his life, to help and bless unnumbered women through all time.

They are as she was, the lady of the far-away ages, who had one son, the darling of her heart, but he died in a sudden disaster; and when the shepherd, who had seen the disaster from afar, came into her presence and said, "Lady, what is good for a bootless bene?" she answered, "Endless sorrow." For she saw in his eyes what he had not the heart to tell her, that her darling was dead; and then she said, "Many a poor man's son shall be rich through my loss and glad through my sorrow." So it was, and this was the fruitage of her tarrying; and so we may see how we may go forth weeping, bearing precious seed, to return again rejoicing, bringing our sheaves with us,— the sheaves of the winter wheat,— when,

> "Beneath the dark November sky,
> With the cold rain falling drearily,
> The seed on the land is cast;
> And in the furrows the grain doth lie
> Till the wintry months be past.

Sown in the cold, dark, desolate days,
Reaped in the sunshine's mellow haze :
Thus in the deep and wond'rous ways
Of God are the lives of men,—
Sorrow and loss, defeats and delays,
Like the storms that nurture the grain.
That which was sown in wintry air
Shall blossom and ripen when skies are fair,
Though thine shall be many an anxious care
Ere the harvest be gathered in.
So be strong to do, and patient to bear,
For the heart that is true shall win."

SEEING GOD AFTERWARD.

"Thou shalt see me afterward, but my face shall not be seen."
Exodus xxxiii. 23.

When the man Moses uttered this prayer, he was passing through a great and sore crisis in his life. He had been forty days alone, as we read, in the fastnesses of Horeb, brooding over the things which took shape finally in the ten commandments; and, as he communed with God in the solitude, a divine inspiration touched him, as he believed, and as I believe, to cast them into this form and set on them the seal of the divine sanction.

That such a stroke of work should have cost him very dear and lifted him high is no wonder; and so we are told that, when he came down from the mountain, his face shone with the light which is not of the sun. But he came down only to find that the tribes he had fought for so bravely and loved so well had fallen back into the gross idolatry from which he had done all in his power to deliver them.

This was a fearful blow to him, no doubt; and we must not wonder that the spirit in him, strung to its utmost tension and worn out with the long fasting, should break out into a mighty rage, in which he burned up their golden calf, ground the cinders to powder, defiled the wells with it, made the leaders in the revolt drink the bitter waters, and served them right. But, when all this was done, a reaction set in; and he went up into the mountains again, quite broken down, as it seems, and in sore doubt whether it was of any use trying to do any more for his people.

And this is the time touched in my text. The assurances which had made his heart so strong aforetime were like music which has lost its melody. The great deliverance had been wrought to no true purpose, while he was waiting again for the voice which had inspired and directed him from the days of the burning bush; but as yet there was no voice for him, and no vision, only clouds and a darkness which seemed to hide God away, as if a web was woven across the sky.

I think it was very much like our own case on some sad November day, when the vault which bends over the spirit seems for the time to be as bleak as that which bends over the world, and our hopes and strivings are like the leaves we are beating into the mire under our feet; and so it was that he wanted what we all want, when we are in this sore stress of the soul, and life grows dark in the shadows touched with despair. He wanted the very present sense and sight of God, which would burn through the darkness and dismay once for all, and set his soul singing of her confidence, as a lark sings far up in the heavens on a fair June morning. Then he could go back to his life and his work again down there in the desert as law-giver and leader, no matter what might befall. And so he cries, "I beseech thee, shew me thy glory."

But there is no worth to me, as I watch him standing there, in the thought that Jehovah cares no more for this cry than the great sphinx cared for those who would bend and pray before her stone-dead presence on the Nile. I love to believe that the heart of Him who pitieth his children yearned over the sorrow-stricken man, and the Father said in his heaven: "I would love to do this for you if it was the best, but this cannot be. I must put you, for your own sake, in the cleft of the rock, cover you with my hand, and narrow down all your seeing to the place where you stand when I pass by; but, then, you shall know this: that it is my hand which has placed you there, and covers you in. And then, when it is dark all about and above you, I will still be near, and nearest when it is darkest; and you shall see me afterward."

This is to me the true interpretation of the passage between the man and the Most High, the child and the Father, in the dim old days; while, once more, to me there is nothing literal in the report as it stands, or objective, as we say, beyond this of the man standing there, and crying out to God in his great and sore trouble.

I have heard how they pretend to show you still the very cleft in which he was hidden; but to me the only reality about it all is very much that you would find if you went to look for Bunyan's Slough of Despond near the dungeon by Bedford Bridge.

It is a report sent down to us touching one of the grandest and most pregnant truths we can ever take to our own hearts in our own personal experience, and then, not in this alone; for we may find the same truth in the highest and broadest revelations of his eternal providence, that we see him afterward rather than there and then, in the processes of nature and the life of the race and the nations, as well as in our own.

And in our own life, when this befalls us, we may feel as this man Moses did that we should be able to go right on with a high heart, and strong, if He, the Holy One, would reveal his presence to us beyond all doubt or question, while we must break down and give up if we cannot behold this glory. Yet all he will or can do for us there and then will be to put us in the cleft of the rock, and cover us with his hand while he passeth by; but, then, the day comes for us, also, when we can see how the darkness has nurtured a faith which that we desire might have slain, as the darkness in which they must be hidden nurtures the roots and seeds of all things, and causes them to bloom forth into the fair glory of the summer.

In the processes of nature, I said, this truth may be found first of all, and the creation of the world, in which the invisible things of him, as Paul says, are clearly seen, being set forth by the things which are made.

For, when we feel our way through the measureless eras which reach inward and downward toward the central fires, we can be well aware, at every step we take, how poor and dim our sense of the divine presence and providence must have been if we could have seen what was done while the Creator was bending over those retorts and furnaces, storing up the rocks and minerals, brooding over the savannahs and seas, and calling forth the swarms of living creatures which were all to take life and life's worth from his hand, and then to pass away.

What does it mean, we should have said,—this life which is forever drifting down to death? Why do these forests stand in the sun, to be torn up by the tornadoes and buried by the convulsions which are forever shaking the world? Why do these fires burn and these waters swirl? and why are the swarms of living creatures sent, shuddering, back to the dust? What does it all mean? Who can watch these things that are made, and believe God is also watching, and holding such a world in the hollow of his hand? This would have been the fruitage of our seeing; but now the time has come,— the great and wonderful afterward.

Man comes forth in the full time to make this world his home; and then, slowly, but surely, the truth begins to grow clear touching the creation. These forests stood in the sun, through the untold ages, that they might store up his fires, while the tornadoes and convulsions hid them away until the time came to reveal them; and untold precious things came forth from the retorts and furnaces, also to bide their time. Nothing lay outside the boundaries of his kingdom in the creation,

> "Not a worm was cloven in vain,
> And not a moth with vain desire
> Was shrivelled in a fruitless fire,
> Or but subserved another's gain."

Now we can see what hand shaped and moulded the foundations of the world. The pebble at our feet tells the story, the coal in our fires, the treasures in our mines, the marble gleaming in the palaces, the very whitewash on our cottage walls. He has taken his hand away from the cleft in the rock, and we see him afterward.

Or shall we notice, again, how this great and noble verity may come home to us in the advent of our human race?

The elders who hear me can well remember the storm brewed and blown from our pulpits and presses when geology came into our courts, and began to question, with bated breath, the interpretations that had been given, time out of mind, touching the creation of the world in six proper days,— say some six thousand years ago. "They were rank infidelity," they cried, "these oppositions of science, falsely so called, to the holy truth: they were the spawn of the pit." Well, that storm has long since blown itself out, and we are rapidly forgetting that there ever was one.

And now, in these later years, here is another blowing from the same quarter over the advent of man. Gleams of light growing from dim toward the dawn are coming to us, from which we begin to be aware of this,— that the race also has been in the cleft of the rock, with the darkness all about and above, and these truths we are to find, which touch the *ascent* of man, are in the divine order which built up the planet from the fires and fogs of the most primitive eras to the glory we witness in the summer tide, from the old red granite to the June roses, and from the monsters of the early world to the orioles and the thrushes brooding and singing over their nests.

So, while we may still say, "It doth not yet appear

what we have been, any more than it appears what we shall be, as we wait for the afterward here and yonder," to me these glimpses and glances toward the truth of the advent of the human race seem like the music in the grand oratorio of the "Creation," which begins with a clash and clang of discords, reaching upward toward the enthralling melodies of heaven.

We must not fear, therefore, what the students in this science may have to tell us for the truth on this question, or the cry of heresy and infidelity from the old quarter, which is growing fainter with every year; for, if they have caught the true thread of the maze and mystery, the truth they still have to tell us will not be alone a revelation of the past, but a glorious prophecy of the future of man. Because, if we were by no means set in the dim and far beginning on the summit of

> "The great world's altar-stairs
> That slope through darkness up to God,"

but began at the lowest base to climb, step by step, from where we were then to where we are now, we may well believe we are still climbing, and shall keep on until we reach the throne.

We must harbor no fear about this man-child of God, whose whole record so far is strewn with the broidery of the golden word "success." And I feel free to confess that it is the far more welcome truth to me to believe that I sprang from a monad,— whatever that may be,— which held its own down there in the cleft, and struck for something better because a divine pang touched it,— struck for something better, and kept on striking,— than it is to believe in him we hear of, who was set in the beginning on the summit, and thence came down headlong, dragging untold myriads in his fall down to "darkness, death, and long despair." Between a man like that and a monad, give me the monad.

So it is not retrospect alone, but prophecy, also, we touch through these intimations of the race in the cleft of the rock. We may well believe we are but a few steps on our way up the ladder which reaches from earth to heaven; but we are climbing age by age,— for this is our doom and our glory,— and so well the great apostle says, "The whole creation groaneth and travaileth in pain together until now." And not only they but ourselves also, which have the first-fruits of the spirit, — even we ourselves groan within ourselves, waiting for our adoption,— to wit, the redemption of our body; for we are saved by hope. But hope that is seen is not hope; for what a man seeth, why doth he yet hope for? But, if we hope for that we see not, then do we with patience wait for it, in the hope that the creation itself also shall be delivered from the bondage of corruption into the glorious liberty of the children of God.

I would notice how this is the truth, once more, touching the nations and the times when they are in the cleft of the rock. Napoleon tears Germany limb from limb in the early years of our century, crushes Berlin under his heel, and covers Prussia as with a pall. The genius of the great German manhood is in the cleft of the rock, where she can see no face of God; but out of that cleft the strong manhood comes forth to do its destined work. Bismarck was born there, the greatest statesman since Cromwell and Von Moltke and the good William, the Emperor.

The German manhood grew great and masterful in the darkness, as she must, or her great day was a thing of the past. She had sunk so low that she was worshipping not one golden calf, but a host of them; and then the new manhood which was to grind these to powder came out of the darkness and the cleft.

I mind how I grew curious once about "The Watch on the Rhine," and wanted to catch its secret of power over the German heart all about us. So I said one day to a master in music, "Play for me, please, your national melody on the great organ, and shake the church with it, if you can." We were alone in the church; and I noticed how his face flushed and his eyes shone as he answered, "I will try," and then how for a few moments he seemed to be dreaming while he touched the keys; and then how the mighty chords began to fill and flood the place, so that, at last, it seemed as if Miriam was singing the song of Moses for the deliverance of Israel from the thrall. It was the music of the new manhood led out of the cleft and reaming with the new life. There was no face of God for Germany when those dark days were on her, but she saw him afterward.

And as it was with Germany, so it was with France in her turn, when liberty turned to libertinism under the usurper, and she fell down and worshipped the golden calf. And what a calf that was, to be sure! It was the time for her true manhood to abide in the cleft. There was no hope for France wallowing in the slough of the Second Empire. But now we begin to see that the divine hand was over and about her in the dark days when her beautiful capital was invested all about; and she is coming forth now to reveal a nobler life than she has ever known since she was a nation, because France also holds a treasure in her heart of a priceless worth to the world,—a genius unique as it is beautiful at its best among the nations of the earth.

So it was again when we went after a cotton calf, and had to swallow the bitter burnt ashes of our nation's idol. We were in the cleft, then, with our father Abraham, with the darkness about and above him; while he must wonder in his good, patient heart when the darkness would pass away.

The light came for us when he made his great Proclamation and the flag was unfurled for freedom and the integrity of the whole nation, the image of God in ebony as in ivory. Then the waters of our Jordan began to part for us this way and that, and we came to our rest. Not more surely did God put the man Moses into the cleft than he put the man Abraham Lincoln there; and not more surely was he with his son in the old time, when he said, "Get thee up into the mountain," and showed him the promised land he must not enter, standing in the sunlight of the new and better time, than he was with our great leader when his work was done and he was swept away suddenly to his rest, when the arm of the assassin was transformed into the chariot of fire.

And so, I think, we come through glimpses and glances such as these to bring this truth of the cleft home, and see what lessons we can learn from it when the darkness is above us, and the walls about us, and we cry also, "I beseech thee, shew me thy glory."

Nor can we do better, as my thought runs, than to cleave still to the Sacred Book for our first lesson of help and heartening, and notice how it came to be the proudest boast of Israel, "We have Abraham to our father"; while such light as shines on his life for us now reveals a man often in the cleft of the rock,— a man who must be content to catch glimpses of God's presence through the crevices and crannies of a dream, and in watching the signs of the sacrifice, because there is no sure word for him and no open vision, and who came wandering from afar in the faith that the land of promise lay at the end of his quest.

For had not the assurance come right from the mouth of God that he should possess the land, and his children should be as the sands on the seashore and as the stars for multitude, to find that the whole worth of the promises had dwindled down at last to a son, getting well on in years, who had not the pluck in him, and courage, to break away from the tents and the mother's apron-string to find the maiden who was to be his wife?

And here, again, is the divinest life the world has ever held, which shines from the eyes and beats in the heart of Jesus Christ. But, if that light had shone on our world then as it shines now, think you that Peter would have blasphemed and told the lie when the damsel said, "This man also was with him," or Judas betrayed him with a kiss, or Pilate have condemned him, for all their clamor? I tell you nay. They would have borne him on their hearts as the most blessed revelation of God's face that had ever come to men. No diadem would have been too rich wherewith to crown him, and no purple too royal for his robe. They would have knelt to do him homage as he walked about the streets; while the high-priest would have met him at the temple gates, and prayed him to enter the most holy place, that the lights on the golden candlesticks might burn forever with a clearer lustre, and the glory on the wings of the cherubim be like that of the angels of the presence nearest the throne.

And this light which shines now from his Gospels, is it not wide as the world and high as heaven? Yet he also was in the cleft, as he hung there on the cross and cried, "My God, my God, why hast thou forsaken me?" And yet unto him also came the divine worth of the darkness, when he never imagines for an instant that he can forsake God.

And so I might go on to tell you how this is the truth touching the most royal souls who have come to help and hearten us in all time. There was not a man or a woman of them all who had not to stand in the cleft of the rock, longing to see God's face, to catch some glimpse, if no more, of the grand, luminous, infinite truth, that they might go right on with never a doubt or fear. What they wanted through the light came to them by the darkness, when all they had to hold them was their faith in the unseen. Yet this was to them as when the sun touches a seed far down in a crevice in the massive walls of some temple of the old idolatries, where the seed grows and burgeons and becomes a thing so mighty that the walls split and shudder down, and the idols follow the idolatries into the dust.

So in our own life the time comes to us all who are

alive unto God when we must stand in the cleft, with the walls of hindrance all about, and the darkness above and before. Yet these may be among the very choicest days in all our life, the days when we make a nobler faith our own.

> "And He is with us in the night
> Who makes the darkness and the light,
> And dwells not in the light alone."

So, if I have touched the truth, what better can befall us than that we should also be set in the cleft, and be brave there and patient, that we may learn the holy lesson the noblest and best have had to learn?

We also may long and cry then to see God's face, and say to ourselves: "One moment of such clear vision would carry us also through the wilderness, singing, to our rest. But it is all so dim we would have so clear," we say; "and what shall we do?" Dim, *dim!* Well, so it was with the planet, with the race, with the nations, and the seers and saints. They all had to wait for the great and sure Afterward in so many ways. Why, then, should not we wait as those that wait for the morning, and nourish through all doubt and dismay our faith in his presence and in the blessedness of the overshadowing hand?

And take the truth of it all to our hearts, finally, for the work God has given us to do as his witnesses and apostles of the broad and sunny faith we love. It is the old cry of the apostle here that we have not already attained, and the brand we have borne, that there is nothing clear and well defined in our beliefs as there is in those of other churches, no creed worth the name which embodies them, and I know not what besides, and do not care to ask. Well, let it be true that we are in the cleft of the rock until now. Then, if we are faithful, we shall come forth as a church of the living God, strong to do his work in this world, and help bring in his kingdom. We cannot see his face, but we shall see him afterward. We are in the clasp of the holy law.

THE JOY IN HARVEST.

"The joy in harvest."—ISAIAH ix. 3.

THERE is no time in the year more welcome to some of us than the fall. We find our sense of its charm grows deeper as the years steal on toward our own November, and the setting in of winter in our human life, because our love for this fair world changes as we change, and stands true to all the seasons.

And so my very earliest memories are those of a child's delight in the early spring, when we went out to find the first snowdrops and the willow blooms that glorify Palm Sunday, and after these the primrose and cowslip, in the old mother land, with the hawthorn, the apple-blossom, the golden gorse, and the early wild rose. The spring-time struck the first note of joy; and then, as my own youth passed away, the summer tides ran through my heart, deep answering unto deep, as they do in us all when our mother Nature has her way with us and we live close to her heart.

And, then, it was the fall; but here I found dismay,— not as yet in the season, for I was not there only in the anticipation.

I had fallen in with the thought that Nature grows sick in the fall, and the pillars of fire she lifts in the woods are the hectic flush which warns us that the end is near. So I had imagined until on one rare day I fell in with a saint and seer a good deal older than I was then. It was a day when this flush and flame pervaded the woods and wild uplands; and so I began to talk in the old sad fashion about this sight, and cited proof from the Scriptures touching the life of man, as, "We all do fade as a leaf." But the old seer was in the fall himself then, while I was still in the summer, and opened another argument drawn from his own experience. "I used to think very much as you do," he said, "when it was the summer-time with me; but now I love to believe that this season is the ripe splendor and glory of the year, and not the dissolution, but the consummation, of all things, when we look well into the heart of Nature through the glass of the good providence of God."

It was a lesson for a lifetime. As these autumn days come with their message to us all, when the time is ripe for the flaming banners to flash out and all things have come to their fine and full perfection that are true to the time, we may say, also, "These are not the signs of dissolution, but of consummation, and not a threnody of death, but a psalm of life, when the mornings are silvered by the breath of the early frosts, and the flowers in our gardens seem like cups of fire which hold all the glory of the spring and the summer in their heart, and the air holds a golden mist and fragrance exhaled from the flowers, the fruits, and the harvest store.

In the spring the world all about us wakes up, and rises to welcome the new day; but the winter dies hard on our zone, and we often ask each other whether this year there will be any spring worth the name. And through the summer the green things growing have to fight stern battles for their life. It is too dry, and they will wither on the stem. It is too wet, and they will rot in the furrows. The blight is on the berry, and the sting is in the plum. The apples are shaken down in the strong winds, and the roots in the gardens are in peril from the evil things that burrow in the dark, mildew and rust is in the air; and the good man on the farm fears for his wheat, or wonders how the corn will fare in the early frosts, or is aware how the soft rains may turn to bullets of ice in the very heart of August, or the canker-worm may eat what the locust has left.

But now the fall comes when the long fight is over, and we know once more there is seed for the sower and bread for the eater. The grapes are full of new wine, and the barns bulge with the fruits of the harvest. The word of the Lord has come true: "I will fill thee with the fine wheat." He has watered the hills from his chambers, and the earth is satisfied with the fruit of his hands. He has caused the grass to grow for the cattle, and the herb for the service of man. We are at one with the wise old husbandman they told me about over the water, who farmed much land and never found fault with the seasons, but would tell you how he had noticed in his many years that what we call a bad season for one thing was good for another.

So we say, if the true heart is in us when the fall comes round: "The divine Husbandman has been helping us, and working with us, stroke for stroke. This small planet of ours has been swinging through her orbit on no mild adventure. The wind, blowing where it listeth, has still been as the breath of the Most High; and his hand hath opened the chambers of heaven, and distilled the rains.

Let the year fall on sleep now: she has wrought nobly, and deserves her rest. This is the consummation: the trees aflame with gold and crimson, and the flowers, are the tokens to us that there is no more death, but a change from glory to glory, as by the spirit of the Lord." And so I love the fall now, when I am in it, for the message of the consummation we find in its heart, which holds the promise of another spring, when

> "Earth is full of heaven,
> And every common bush afire with God."

It deepens and widens our joy, once more, to believe how much greater the harvest of God is, who satisfieth the desires of every living thing, than this we reckon on and weigh and measure for our own. "It will be a hard winter," ancient men say, who live on the land: "see what a wealth of things are ripening for the birds and the squirrels." The foretelling does not always come true; but I like to hear them say so, because it reveals a certain faith in the heart which dwells with these things, which looks toward the promise, "As thy day is, so shall thy strength be," and which reaches away down to the sparrow, and makes him our commentator for the divine lesson in the Sermon on the Mount,—that every bird has his own provision and the harvests of heaven reach from pole to pole.

In the early days in Virginia they offered a bounty for killing the crows, because they ate up the new-sown seed. So the creatures fled into the wilderness for dear life, and waited on God's hand; and then in no long time the Assembly offered a bounty to get them back again, because it had become a question of no crow, no corn. They were watchmen, when the whole truth came out, and must have their wages.

And John Burroughs says, "The lark I was looking at the other day has a brain one-third larger by proportion with his body than Shakspere or Webster." It is the pledge that the great mother will see to her nurslings by fitting them forth so handsomely to see after themselves.

"We do not suspect," Darwin says, again, "how ignorant we are of the conditions of existence among the creatures on which we are in the habit of looking down"; but we may all learn something, as we see how he the old saga calls the First Provider gives them all their meat in due season, and think how the harvest on which they rely has ripened day by day with ours. It ripens for them from the Iceland moss to the palm-trees on the equator.

The boys race with the squirrels for the nuts, and the birds for the berries. There is plenty for them all, and to spare. The King's messengers are among the highways and hedges, bidding the poorest and most forlorn to the feast; and all living things are bound up in the bundle of life with him, while man has only the pre-eminence and distinction of keeping order within the boundaries of his own commonwealth, and then the holy Providence sees to the rest by nature's ample laws.

So nothing is made in vain, I say, when I touch

the truth of the noble consummation; and nothing is made in vain. The Canada thistle is as beautiful and good in its own proper place as the rose of Sharon. And what a loathsome creature is your crocodile! What an uproar there would be if one was found in any of the great reservoirs, whence the water flows into the homes of our cities! They tell me they care for them as constantly in the reservoirs in Ceylon as our fine ladies care for those deplorable lap-dogs, because the water, under their fervid sun, would slay them but for the crocodile.

It is a hint, and no more, of the great harvest of God, which rounds and ripens through all the world, and holds within its zones a touch of his own infinity. There are creatures which need a forest for food and house-room. There are hosts I cannot see living within the cup of a lily or a violet. "These all wait on him, and he giveth them their meat in due season"; and all's right with the world when we are right in it. Why should we grow sad, then, when the golden glow falls about us in these autumn days, like a garment woven in celestial looms?

It may well deepen and widen our joy, again, to think what a wealth of difference and distinction comes with this matchless bounty, and how it all answers to a need or ministers to a delight.

I had a dear friend once who would have nothing to do with the strawberries which came to us in the winter, because, he held, they must ripen within a degree of his own garden, and in the sun, while they were only at their best when you can pluck them from your own vines. And, wandering with him once in the Old World, I noticed he would only eat what wholesome people were eating, where we went, and drink, as a rule, what they were drinking. "We drop in on a visit," he would say, "but they have been here time out of mind, learning what was good for them from the good mother Nature, and taking it from her hand." It was his way of touching the difference and distinction which lies along all the latitudes and longitudes, his conception of the trees of life, the seer saw, which yield their fruit every month, and whose leaves are for the healing of the nations.

They tell us the apple has never been found within the tropics of its own free will, or the orange where you can cut ice, and each is the match for the man who lives here or yonder. "What do you miss in your fruit?" I said once to a friend who lives far away to the southward. "The snap and tang of the winter," he answered. He was raised in Massachusetts; but the native man down there would never have made that answer.

We fight stern battles for our harvest stores, and win a wealth of sturdy manhood with them, which is making us the rulers of the world; but the children of the soft and sunny climes fight no such battles, and even the ants, where the sun is most fervid, turn their backs on Solomon. They will do nothing in the glare of the day, or lay up stores for the winter which never comes. The bread fruit, the palm, and the banana grow almost without a thought or care. The thinking is of close kin to the demand. The great domed brain of a man like Webster is never nourished forth on the bread fruit and the palm. The salmon will only haunt cold waters: he is the match and marrow of cold weather.

We can exchange what we have for what they have, and so enlarge the boundaries of worth and enjoyment, but the main truth is this: that each zone reveals the wonder of bread enough, and then of the bread the man needs who dwells there, or he could not stay; and the saying of the prophet comes forever true: "I will hear the heavens," saith the Lord, "and the heavens shall hear the earth, and the earth shall hear the corn and wine and oil, and they shall hear Jezreel,"—the sown of God.

It is the next great joy, then,—this of the difference and distinction in which all his gifts are as the bread which cometh down from heaven; and how well our children answer to this law, who rebel against a gray monotony even of good things, when in our foolish wisdom we would shut them up in some theory or dogma we have stolen from a book perchance, done by a man who has quite forgotten his own childhood, or had none worth the name!

The joy of harvest should grow deep and radiant in all our hearts, again, when we think of the bounty and blessing it brings to the nations as well as to our own home land.

The sun shines on no home within the American republic where there may not be bread enough, and to spare, if the bread-winner will see to it, and quit himself like a man; nor is there any home where the bread-winner is disabled or dead in which there will not be bread enough, when the need is once made known; while in the Old World there is hardly a poor man's platter on which you shall not find what is to him a new plenty, because of the ploughman and herdsman of these States. And so the ploughman and herdsman, as good Jeremy Taylor says, are also ministers of God.

The long sad cry of the poor for bread is stayed now, as it never was before, especially in our own mother lands; and we are God's bread-winners and bread-breakers for the nations. But woe to us if we do not find some way to meet and master the shameful things which are done so often, through which every poor man's loaf is made lighter and our fair commerce shamed!

In the lawless ages they followed

> "The good old rule, the simple plan,
> That he shall take who has the power,
> And he shall keep who can."

They would swoop down from their strongholds then and take toll of the merchants as they went on their way to the markets; and they must submit, because might made right. We call the strongholds a "corner" now or a syndicate or a trust; but the things they do are often no better, and I wish I could believe not seldom they are no worse.

Still, the truth abides that our land is flooded with plenty. There is seed for the sower, and bread for the eater. He who ruleth in the heavens hears the cry of all the creatures of his hand; and to all he not only giveth meat in due season, but the due meat. We can help the world, while still we help ourselves; and, if we stand true to the holy law of neighbor to neighbor and man to man, we can make the whole world brighter by our bounty, and cause it to rejoice in our joy.

And, then, we may well ask once more what truth these things, which are seen and temporal, can bring home to us all, touching the things which are unseen and eternal, and find this among the first we have glanced at for an instant already,—that this world of ours swings on in no blind fashion, but is held to its course by the hand of the Most High.

A fearful thing it is, indeed, to think of this home of ours threading its way among the constellations, balancing itself between the sun and the infinite dark void, and of the imprisoned elements, and what would befall if they broke loose utterly; for where would these autumn glories be then, with the harvests and homes, and with them this marvellous human creature, man, He has made a little *higher* than the angels, and crowned with glory and honor?

It is only fearful, and food for any sad foreboding, when we leave out of the reckoning His divine presence and providence who cares not for the worlds alone, but for the lily and the sparrow, and touched me with a pang of delight long ago, when I saw the bluebells on the crest of the Rhigi balancing themselves against the whole solar system, swinging free in the fresh wind of the morning, wet with the rain and resplendent in the sun.

This earth of ours is true to her seasons because God is true and steadfast to his divine purpose and plan, from whom all things spring, as the fountain springs from the great deeps, and has made no mistake in his making or lost any thread in the guiding. Let us be sure of that, as we rejoice before him in the joy of harvest. It has never been a lost world, but found rather to a diviner purpose always, and was never so radiant with his presence as it is this morning.

We may lay this truth also to our hearts as we grow glad for the harvest home: that, while my joy and yours rests in him, it rests also in its own due measure with us, as all joy must. We have to win by good, honest striving. All the harvest homes worth the name are the fruit of such striving, as well as of the help of God. I know about where to look for the poor, scant harvests a thousand miles from where I stand, and I know the reason, which must still be guarded by Paul's tender caution, who made thee to differ, why there is an abounding grace there, and yonder only disgrace; and this truth lies within the whole sum and substance of our life.

All the harvests are ours for the striving; and do not you forget that, especially, who are in the spring-time of what you may be and do. We may have a poor lot to work on: it need not stay poor, if we add to our faith virtue. We may think we are poor sticks. So the poor stick of a willow might have said, my friend left on the edge of a marsh and thought no more about it. But the wetness touched the dry thing, and the sun and the rain fell on it, so tiny spikelets shot forth when the spring came; and, when he took me to see it after many years, there was a grand bole, and waving banners of green, and the birds were nesting and singing far aloft for joy of the tree.

I love to think of another truth these golden days bring home to us all,— the truth that some fruits ripen early and some late; and some flowers shed their white glory in the spring, while some endure right on to the frosts of winter, for this is the law of their diverse life. Yet how rich the year is through the whole wealth of them, the bounty, the beauty, and the fragrance! And so shall we not think of the ingathering of the harvest of heaven and the angels "All too soon," we moaned, "all too soon! Why must they be taken?" But the blessed truth remains that we had them once, and have them still. They are our treasures laid up in heaven. They did come to bless us,—the fair fruits and flowers of the spring-time and the summer; and we can sing with the great singer, then,—

> "This truth came borne with bier and pall,
> I felt it when I sorrowed most,
> 'Tis better to have loved and lost
> Than never to have loved at all."

And one last word for the charity that never faileth. How forbidding some of the good fruits of the harvest are on the surface! How sweet and good in the heart! And how evil a thing it would be to judge them only by what we see, or to judge them before their time!

The fall days come, the frost mellows them, or you get at the heart of your hard shell; and then how sweet and good they are, to be sure! It is of men like Milton they remind us, and Johnson or Stephen Girard, and hosts of men besides we may have known, who needed all the sun there was, and a touch of the frost, too. And, then, that time should shred away the shell, the sweetness lay not on the surface: it was deep in the heart, guarded by the knots or the spikes. I say we have all known such men, hard and angular or sharp to our touch as a chestnut-burr; and there would have been no great worth, perhaps, if we had broken through the shell before the time.

I made one of these some amends when he was dead, but still repent me of my harsh judgment while he was alive. No man more honest, but he seemed to be all hard shell; and then men came to me and told me of things he had done in the later years, and done in secret, the angels of God might envy. Then I said in my heart, "If I am worthy to meet that man in heaven, when I get through down here, I will beg his pardon"; and I still mean to do it. It was the hard shell or the chestnut-burr I was scolding and fretting about, and wist not of the sweet and shining heart.

Yes, and let these days teach us some good lessons of faith and hope for those that seem to our poor seeing to hold no worth in them at all. Long ago I would be busy in my overtime among the flowers, and got some seed one spring of a rare and unique sort to sow and raise a wealth of beauty and fragrance from my seeds. But the soil was not good, and the sun came late on that side the house, so the promise did not come true. Still, a cup or so did flash forth into beauty and grace; while, when the frosts came, I found a seed or two in the wreck of my hope, and said: "I will save these for another summer, and try again. These seeds are the proof there will be another summer, if we had no other proof." So the spring came, when, having learned something by my failure, I set them in a richer tilth that lay fairer to the sun; and, lo! my flowers were the glory of my garden.

It is the everlasting gospel of the grace of God

which touches our whole life. Not a plant or flower in his garden just like another, and no best without a better hanging in the heavens we must capture and bring down.

Yes, and the soil, how harsh and poor it is for some! and the sun, how late he shines for some! and the things that stab and sting, how cruel they are to root and stalk in some! And then we say, "What a wreck!" But this is God's husbandry as well as ours. "All souls are mine," saith the Lord; and if we will but turn to him, as my poor flower turned to what sun there was, and make the best of the harsh and poor soil in which our life may be set to grow, then there shall be a seed saved and sown again for the

> "Immortal life in never failing worlds,
> For mortal creatures conquered and secure."

THE RICH AND THE POOR.

"The rich and the poor meet together. The Lord is the maker of them all."—PROVERBS xxii. 2.

I TAKE it to be beyond all question true that there has been no time when the richer man and woman hood in this land has been so eager as it is now to make this true, that, because the Lord is the Maker of us all, those who are rich in fortune or endowment must do what lies in their power to lift their poorer brothers and sisters toward some better eminence than that on which they stand in the republic.

A wise and good man, who rose to great eminence at the English bar, said, when he was far on in life, "Every year I live shows me more clearly that we give far too poor a meaning to the word 'brother,' and so fail in our true sympathy for the multitudes we call our fellow-citizens." And this is still true, no doubt, here and in my mother land. Many do not care to nourish such a sympathy, or look down on the poor with dislike and disdain; while many more, who are eager to do what they can to bridge the chasm are at a loss how to begin. Still, much is done now, as it was never done before, for proof and prophecy.

For as one of my small grandsons, just a mite of a boy, would draw himself up now and then to far more than his full stature by the measure of the man that lay within him,—and invite me to feel the bulge on his arm, the proof to his fond old grandsire of his desire to loom up as large as the pattern he saw in the mount, so, when we see this striving in the nobler manhood and womanhood of our land to grow up into Him who is our living head in this sympathy, that they may inform and inspire their poorer brothers and sisters, and help them in all wise and gracious ways to come up higher, this is the proof and prophecy that we shall also grow up to "the measure of the man," as the seer has it,— "that is, of the angel."

This is the more welcome and good, again, to hear of and see, when we notice what a wide and true interpretation we are giving to this term "the poor," and what wise and true ways we are devising by which we may slip something of the wealth the well-endowed or the well-to-do possess into their life, so that they may rise to the fairer eminence in life and fortune.

The time was with us, as it was with the world all about us, when we did not meet together, as the waters meet and blend to fill some great river,— the rich and the poor,—but were as the streams which flow onward, each in its own proper channel, and seek no alliance. Or the rich and the poor might be thrown together, as they must be, but it was very much as the icebergs are thrown together, when they drift down to the southward.

They might be touched here and there in the kindly sun of this human sympathy, so that some cube from each would meet and blend; but the solid substance of the bergs would abide as they were until they vanished in the sea of the eternal life. The poor in fortune, or in moral and mental endowment, so that they could not breast the tides like strong swimmers, but must drift back and forth like logs, to be thrown on the sand and rot or be burned,— as the stern old dogma ran,— this was the station in our life unto which they were called,— these poor; and with that they must be content, because it was the will of God concerning them, and was made good by the words of the Master and Lord: "The poor ye have always with you."

And so, when the sifted and right good seed began to grow down there to the eastward, and the great and holy truth the Master tells in his parable of the sower began to take shape and form in human lives, and some seed fell in the good ground to bring forth the forty, sixty, and a hundred fold,— some on the poor ledge, where there was no deepness; some on the gross and unclean spaces, where the thorns sprang up and choked it; and some by the wayside, where it was presently devoured,— great-hearted as many of them were in spots, the heart in them was not great enough to take home this truth,— that one hand lay behind all the sowing, the hand of the Lord and Maker of them all.

And so there were God's poor among them, and then their own. Those who had no hope in their life, because they were not men, but the frustrations of men, or men who did come to some poor and poverty-stricken caring of fivefold, shall we say, against the hundred in the rich, deep loam,— these were God's poor, or their own.

But below these there was the low-down sowing, which had come up among the thorns and briars in the sour haulms of our human life; and these, as we can easily see, were to them the devil's poor, for which they found it hard to say even the prayer of the good Scotch Calvinist of a later day: "Lord, let them hang ower hell, but dinna let them fall in." They let them fall in, whatever He might do whose mercy endureth forever, and said their end was to be burned.

This was the way we began with these poor down there where the main tap-root of our nation lies. The rich and the poor met together; but they did not meet and blend in a pure and true sympathy. The little band which landed on the rock was poor to the bare bone almost when it began to plant and build; while there were few rich who came westward ten years later, and so far, I suppose, it was one stream of tendency along the whole line of their life. Still, when the sowing began to grow together, toward the harvest, we begin to see the ever-growing distinction between the rich and the poor in the ordering of their life, and then between their own poor and those I have named once for all.

They were instinctive democrats, or the most of them, in thought and purpose; but the well-to-do were social and religious aristocrats, I think in quite an equal measure, from the merchants and selectmen, and the rest of a good degree, to the deacons and elders, and above them all the minister, in his towering pulpit, his wide-flowing wig, with the Geneva gown and bands.

These were the symbols of this separation between the rich and the poor down there,— the hundred-fold ears, the growth on the hungry ledge, and that among the thorns and briars. And so did some hapless man go all wrong, or some woman, like Hester in "The Scarlet Letter," that matchless study of the old grim life, they burned the brand on them where it would stay through all time.

They said every day, on their knees before the God and Father of us all, "Forgive us our trespasses, as we forgive them that trespass against us"; but all the same they felt they must keep a record of those things they could not and would not forgive, though they might well spring from some sore and sad poverty of the moral nature, or some strong passion born of the evil we can so seldom trace in the heavy overgrowth of the thorns and briars.

It did not and, it is but fair to say, could not occur to this splendid manhood and womanhood to add to their virtue knowledge, and so ask whether the low, receding forehead, the weak and slack-twisted mouth and chin, the dangling hands, the shuffling feet, or the sensual mask might not stand for poverty where it may be most ruthless or hopeless, and say: "Now let us bear with these poor, and slip some worth into their life out of the wealth He has given us in mind or moral worth or fortune, not because they are beggars, but brothers before the Lord and Maker of us all. Let us try to put ourselves in their place, and begin by getting down, in our sympathy for them, close to where they stand, that we may the better *understand* them, as He did who said, 'He that will be greatest among you, let him be the servant of all.'"

They had noble and generous impulses,—these old Puritans who started the nation; but we do not find this among them,—to seek and to save that which was lost by reason of the bare, rugged ledge, the sour and weedy space where the drip was, or where there was nothing to get hold of worth the name by reason of the wayside scattering of the seed.

They did maintain their churches nobly and well for those times, and got a schoolmaster there by the rock before they got a regular minister from across the sea, while the poor must not cry for bread with none to hear and help them. This is all true.

But the picture of a later day is drawn from the life by the hand of genius, in which, as you will remember, the good and most capable house mother takes poor, shiftless Sam Lawson, the village blacksmith, to task, and gives him a good sound scolding; while the shambling fellow bears it the best he may, as he sees the Thanksgiving turkey bulge out in brave relief under her apron.

Sam had to be about the man he was, one of God's poor; and once, when I met the peerless woman who has drawn his portrait with so many touches of tender relenting, I thanked her heartily for blending so deftly a ne'er-do-weel with the germ of the saint which may still be born in the line of the swarming household when every winter turns to spring for the poor ears up there on the ledge.

He bears the good scolding the best he may, poor fellow; but there is no humble heart in the good housewife with the question, "Who made me and mine to differ, or how is it that we have the turkey to give, while he must take it with that blush, half of pleasure for the wife's sake and the children, and half of shame for his own?"

Not this question, and no invitation that they shall all come over and spend the day under the radiant rooftree, so that, sitting down on equal terms as near as may be, Sam may perhaps win some touch of a proper pride, and say, "Why, they treat us like their equals, and not as the rich toward the poor; and so now I will try to do better, and, then, who knows whether some day they may not come to eat at our house in return." It was not to be done in this way or thought of,— the chasm was too wide.

They were of the breed from which a true and clean democracy springs; but they were aristocrats in the social order all the same, and could not help it.

And the Majesty of England sent over men of rank and title to live with them and on their substance, but these were never a part of their more intimate life. That life lay with the people, and the people alone; but it was this I would try to touch of the rich and the poor, whose life ran each in its own channel, and so you must be rich in land and beeves, in merchandise and money, or in talent or learning, before you could blend with the finer life, while, if you were of no account, you must stay where you belonged.

Now, I said, we have these still, and it may be in a larger average, to which the manhood of this finer and more gracious turn are only as yet what Matthew Arnold calls the remnant, men and women, who would not lower by a line the middle wall of partition between the rich and the poor, but would make it still higher and stronger, who can never begin to understand these poor, as we should all try to understand them, until they realize how much less of merit there is in their finer fortune or endowment than they imagine, and how much less of demerit there may be in those on whom they look down from their proud pre-eminence, or realize that what they have done for themselves, who stand highest and have done best, is but the token of what He has done for them, who is the Lord and the Maker of us all, through generations of striving it may be, which are lost in the mists of time, while, if they could but scan the whole story as it stands, they might say by grace we are saved from being now among these poorest, and it is not of ourselves,—it is the gift of God.

Are such men as I glance at among the organizers and employers of labor? The head does not say to the hands in this good fashion of sympathy, "I need you just as surely as you need me"; and so, when the bell taps for each and all to go home, they move as far apart in this sympathy as Chippewa is from China.

Or do we establish churches, who are of this type and temper, in his name who is the Maker of us all, and in his name who sat at meat with all sorts and conditions of men in the frankest and sweetest fashion? What are these very often but clubs for the finer and selecter sort, while for the rest there are kitchen churches, shall I say, where we send the broken meats of the ministry, and expect them to be content and thrive?

Do these speak to the poor, their voice is a note or two higher than the tones they use to each other, or half an octave perhaps, than the scale they use for their equals; and so it is with the whole finer life as it touches the poorer, who are not rated at what they are worth to God then, but at their worth to us, if there be any, as the greatest man we can name in his time set store on the simple old farmer, and loved now and then to be with him, but, as I make out, it was as when you open your heart to the saltness of the sea on a fair summer's day, or to the aromatic snap of the uplands thick with wild roses and sweet fern.

This is the old life come to its flowering; but, if this was all, we might well be alarmed, but it is not all. The better and nobler sympathy we find springing forth now is what I thank God for, which is bound to find great and gracious meanings in the words I have read.

The real and true concern in so many whose fortune lies in wealth or endowment is to make their wealth a leaven which will lighten and sweeten the life below them. And I notice this now in my motherland as I never did before.

There the employers who are wise in this wisdom of pure sympathy build sweet and fair homes for what they call their "hands" and libraries and reading-rooms. They will go with them also, if they may now and then, on a day's holiday or have them come to the mansion or the park, and sit down with them at meat.

They are touched by the beautiful contagion, and are trying to even things up a little more all the time, and be more nearly at one with their poorer brothers and sisters. Yet there is no man who sets more store on wealth and station than your Englishman; and old Pepys does but speak for his order, when he writes in his diary, "This day I rode for the first time in my own carriage, at which I lifted my heart to God, and prayed him to continue it."

Now you who came here first have done some grand things for those among us who must come after. You have thrown this goodly land open to the whole world,— excepting China, to our common shame,— so that the poorest man who comes here, if he can and will work, may begin at once to live better than he ever dreamed of living before, and win a good sure future for himself and his family. And with this you have given us all the rights of citizenship far ahead often of our power to use them well, making us all as rich in this endowment as the manhood is which has shed its blood on the battle-fields of two hundred and seventy years.

So you have also created our common school system, built churches, hospitals, and asylums for the sick, the insane, the feeble, the aged, and the poor who have none to help them, and made no distinction worth naming between the new-comer and the home-born man; while these grand universities and libraries are springing far and wide, to which we are all made welcome.

I cannot tell the story, and need not, because we all know it, and know also that this grand lifting of our life from the lower toward the higher planes among those I think of is not done by the derrick, but from the breast. So we may well ask what we can do more than has been and is now being done, that the rich and the poor may meet together in a purer sympathy, because the Lord is the Maker of us all.

I have but one answer to the question; and it springs from the seed of God's grace in us all, if we will mind it, through which we shall all try to enter into the life and fortune of the poor who have no fortune, we can reckon in mind, body, or estate, as we have, and lend them a hand in which there is the pulse of a good human heart, see where we can meet them on the ground of our common human brotherhood; and that's all.

Am I rich in fortune or in some finer wealth of birth and culture, I shall not be afraid, then, that my costly vase will suffer harm or loss by neighboring with the earthen pipkin. I shall remember that in all great houses there be divers vessels; and the pan, brown or black, which will stand the fire and cook the dinner, shall be in no wise counted for dishonor,— no, not even against the vase which might adorn the palace of a king.

I love to muse over the untold worth of a race, and am mighty proud of yours and mine. The yellow-haired, blue-eyed, great-limbed fellow who came storming in from the northward once on a time, and took possession of about all he saw, he is of the manhood to which we belong, which has carried all before it so far in the long, stern fight for the first place among the nations.

The eager desire to be as far up as we are was reaming in the blood; and this whole upward march in two worlds has been on the line of our ambition and delight. It was the gift of God; and we must dree our splendid doom wherever we are, in England, Germany, in these States, and underneath the planet, in Australia.

That is the law which lies within your life and mine. We are rich, while other races I could name are poor, who are blended with our life. But, if He who came to preach the gospel to the poor taught us one truth above another we must never forget, it was this of a real human brotherhood, founded on the holy truth that the Lord is not only the Maker, he is also the Father of us all.

And this truth sank so deep into the hearts of those who were one with him in mind and purpose that it brought the infant Church and the cause it stood for into instant peril, when every man began to strip himself of the fruit of his endeavor, casting everything he possessed into the common treasury, and so opened for the most shiftless and worthless to share, and share alike, if they would only make up a poor and pious face,— which was all a mistake then as it is now, and far from His mind and purpose who said, "Ye have come for the loaves and fishes."

This was what he did who came to seek and to save *that* which was lost. He came closest to those who were poorest, and most utterly lost,— the devil's poor, if you will; and I may say that bad word again,— that he might pour into their forlorn natures some treasure from his own divine life, and so call out what was still divine in theirs.

The devout Persian prays, "O God, do something for the bad: thou hast done everything for the good in making them so good." He was here in God's stead, the dear Son of the All-Father, to minister to these poor with human hands, to reach them through this human sympathy which then became divine, to talk with them humanly and tenderly as man to man and man to woman, and to pour scorn and the wrath of the Lamb on those who stood so high above them, and were as hard in this human touch and sympathy for them as nails, counting the very alms they gave an investment which would return to their own proper profit.

It is the beginning of the gospel of God to the poor in him who came to give sight to the blind, to restore the withered hand, to brace up the hapless will, to bid the lame walk, to command the evil spirit to come out, and to set at liberty them that were bound. Not to leave them in their isolation, but to make them feel there was one in this world who could not and would not let them go stumbling on in the dark, to bruise themselves on the flints which lie on the way of life for us all, but would by all means help them. "Therefore, he who was rich for our sakes became poor, that we through his poverty might be made rich."

So I will end where I began, with a note of joy over the signs and tokens of this sympathy of the rich toward the poor in the line of the holy Gospels, whatsoever form it may take. It is proof and prophecy of the good time coming to me,—

> "When wealth no more shall rest in mounded heaps,
> But smit with freer light shall slowly melt
> In many streams to fatten lower lands,
> And light shall spread, and man be liker man
> Through all the seasons of the golden year."

They told me once, when I went to Niagara, that, when they would bridge the great chasm, they sent a kite over first, and that drew a string. And the string drew a cable which held up a man, who got things started for the superb Suspension Bridge, which helps to clasp the continent together, and holds us all who see it in the spell of its beauty. And so, from these fine threads of human sympathy, these unwindings of the heartstrings and the purse-strings, these wings of a true and tender concern which take us across the chasm between the rich and the poor, we can reach those who by nature or fortune have yet to be where they belong, and win them to believe that any true gospel to them stands, first of all, for the good human brotherhood; and then this must follow, as the spring follows the winter. That those we can reach in this way will be touched by the truth that there is not only a better and nobler life waiting their striving and winning on the earth and in the heavens, but right friendly hearts to feel this sweet concern for them, with hands to clasp theirs and to hide holy meanings they could not dream of in those words as true as they are imperative,—

> "The rich and the poor meet together:
> The Lord is the Maker of them all."

www.ingramcontent.com/pod-product-compliance
Lightning Source LLC
Chambersburg PA
CBHW020900230426
43666CB00008B/1250